D0813378

Reflections from ZORA!

Celebrating 25 Years of the Zora Neale Hurston Festival of the Arts and Humanities

This book created by
The Florida Historical Society
in conjunction with
The Association to Preserve the Eatonville Community, Inc.
(P.E.C.)

Reflections from Zora!
  Celebrating 25 Years of the Zora Neale Hurston Festival
  of the Arts and Humanities

Copyright 2014 by The Association to Preserve the Eatonville Community, Inc. (P.E.C.)

Photographs by Ted Hollins

All rights reserved under International and Pan-American Copyright Conventions. No part of this book may be reproduced in any form or by any means, electronic or mechanical, including photocopying, recording, or by any information storage and retrieval system, without permission in writing from the publisher, except by a reviewer who may quote brief passages in a review.

ISBN: 978-1-886104-68-6

The Florida Historical Society Press
435 Brevard Avenue
Cocoa, FL 32922
www.myfloridahistory.org/fhspress

P•R•E•S•S

Bronze sculpture of Zora Neale Hurston by Brian R. Owens.

Acknowledgements

Like the Zora Neale Hurston Festival of the Arts and Humanities itself, this project would not have been possible without the hard work of dedicated individuals. Thanks are owed to the board of directors, national planning committee, staff, and volunteers of the Association to Preserve the Eatonville Community, Inc. (P.E.C.) for organizing twenty-five years of outstanding presentations that provide most of the content for this book. Particular thanks are owed to Mrs. N.Y. Nathiri, Director of Multidisciplinary Programs for P.E.C. Thanks also to Ted Hollins, the "official" photographer of the ZORA! Festival.

Transcriptions of the taped presentations included in this book were provided by Terry Olsen, Michael Osowski, and Michelle Frank of the Orange County Arts and Cultural Affairs department. Thanks to all of the presenters and essayists whose words are used here. Although every effort has been made to make these spoken word presentations translate effectively into this printed format, readers should note that conversational speaking is, by nature, disjointed and generally less structured than the written word. That conversational style has been preserved here.

At the Florida Historical Society Press, copy editor Kirsten Russell rose to the immense and unique challenges of this project along with assistant copy editor Chris Galloway. Thanks to Chris Brotemarkle for the cover concept and her assistance with editing. As always, thanks to Paul Pruett for his layout and design of the book. Thanks to you, the reader, for your interest in the Zora Neale Hurston Festival of the Arts and Humanities.

Dr. Ben Brotemarkle
Executive Director
Florida Historical Society
January 2014

Table of Contents

Introduction

The Zora Neale Hurston Festival of the Arts and Humanities (ZORA! Festival): Building Community through Pride of Heritage, Educational Excellence and the Cultural Arts

N.Y. Nathiri

Mrs. N.Y. Nathiri is Director of Multidisciplinary Programs for the Association to Preserve the Eatonville Community, Inc. (P.E.C.) From the first event in 1990, N.Y. Nathiri has served as Director of the Zora Neale Hurston Festival of the Arts and Humanities. She is also Director of the Zora Neale Hurston National Museum of Fine Arts, and oversees activities for the Zora Neale Hurston Youth Institute. She is editor and compiler of the book Zora! Zora Neale Hurston: A Woman and her Community *(1991). N.Y. Nathiri grew up in Eatonville and her grandfather, A.N. Johnson, was mayor in the 1930s. She has devoted herself to research, writing, and community education for the town of Eatonville.*

The Association to Preserve the Eatonville Community, Inc. (P.E.C.) was formed during the time between Thanksgiving and Christmas of 1987 in response to the unanimous decision of the Orange County Board of Commissioners to approve a road improvement project which, if completed, would have destroyed the historic character of little Eatonville and which would have left a scar on the Maitland neighborhood of homeowners, apartment dwellers and small businesses who resided along the roadway, leading to U.S. 17-92. Called East Kennedy Boulevard in Eatonville and Lake Avenue in Maitland, this 1.4 mile stretch of road was itself historic, having been known as early as the 1830s as the Old Apopka Highway because it served as the connector between the northeast and northwest sections of the county.

When the Commissioners decided to five-lane the existing two-lane road in Eatonville, they had no knowledge of the community as historically significant; or, that for tens of thousands, Eatonville was a beloved literary destination; and they certainly had not heard of Zora Neale Hurston.

The "First Annual Zora Neale Hurston Festival of the Arts" presented in 1990 by P.E.C. was established to change that reality; and to do so, in an engaging and enjoyable way — a soft approach to a hard problem: How to alter the public's multiple negative perceptions, based upon un-informed, and ill-informed opinions, fundamentally due to a lack of knowledge and exposure.

As we began planning in the Fall of 1988, we determined that the Festival should have three goals: (1) to celebrate the life and work of 20th century writer, folklorist and anthropologist Zora Neale Hurston; (2) to celebrate the historic significance of her hometown, Eatonville, as our nation's oldest incorporated African American municipality; and (3) to celebrate the cultural contributions which people of African ancestry have made to the United States and to world culture.

For a quarter of a century, the ZORA! Festival has addressed these goals by presenting a consistently excellent program of arts and humanities offerings. Our organization is respected for our commitment to host scholars with impeccable credentials and to invite some of our country's most respected artists to the festival stage; and for this achievement, we have been privileged to receive accolades from our peers, at home and beyond.

Yet, there is something else which has been occurring during these twenty-five years: Quiet and powerful, it manifests itself in different guises. One example of this phenomenon is occurring at the "Make and Take Tent," the place where our littlest visitors have fun creating arts and crafts, which are designed to support the classroom curriculum they must master. For the entire twenty-five years of the ZORA! Festival, it has been the women of the Zeta Phi Beta Sorority who have supported the activity with their cash and their time. They now report that we are seeing young teachers, once themselves children visiting the Make and Take Tent, bringing their classes of students to enjoy the same experience they had had in their youth.

Another example is the community of scholars and professionals, mostly women, who have established bonds which go beyond the traditional definition of "networking." In some instances, they speak of life crises which they have survived because of the strength of their Festival sisters. As a part of their yearly routine, they meet the last week in January to enjoy Zora's Eatonville!

Then, there is the oft-heard story of the transplant to Central Florida. In her/his previous community, she/he was accustomed to having a wide variety of cultural options. Feeling that their move to Greater Orlando has disadvantaged them; relegated them to the status of "culturally deprived," they have found solace in ZORA! Festival. They have become energized by volunteering and they have found a quality of intellectual and emotional satisfaction.

There is one other powerful example of the quiet impact ZORA! Festival has had on our peers. For the Twelfth ZORA! Festival (2000), our theme was dance and movement. We presented dance scholars Drs. John O. Perpener, III; Veta Goler; Brenda Dixon Gottschild; and C. S'Thembile West. The Dayton Contemporary Dance Company participated in a multi-day residence; and at our Awards Gala, we honored the late Dr. Katherine Dunham. Shortly after the festival's conclusion, we received a brief handwritten note from a journalist whose assignment was to cover dance for her newspaper. Simply, she stated how grateful she was to ZORA! Festival for bringing to the Central Florida community the quality of programming that we do; that with the dance festival, she had been able to hear public

3

talks and to interact with persons she had wanted to meet all of her professional life.

Candidly, we began the ZORA! Festival as a marketing initiative. We needed to find a way of creating another persona for the Eatonville community. We needed to have decision-makers and opinion-shapers recognize that this little town, "a stone's throw" from Orlando, has the potential to improve qualitatively life, not just for its residents, but for its neighbors as well. As an attractions executive once shared, "All of my creative energies are devoted to trying to develop something special; and every day, as I drive down I-4 from my house, on the way to my job, I pass Eatonville and muse to myself, here's something that does not have to be created; it's already authentic."

As P.E.C. prepares for the next twenty-five years of the ZORA! Festival, what appears to be the true strength of the event is the fact that it has been able to establish a series of strong bonds—bonds which are internal to "Zora's People," as well as bonds among people of different backgrounds, social and economic classes, age groups, and ethnicities. This forging of community through pride of heritage, educational excellence, and the cultural arts can be seen best on "Education Day," always the Friday of the event. There at the Outdoor Festival are children and youth from various heritage groups. They move about briskly and/or they become seriously engaged in some activity. They are peaceable and they are content. For this one day, at least, they embody the beauty of community.

Mrs. N.Y. Nathiri

Students attend Education Day programs

Crowds enjoy vendors at the ZORA! Outdoor Festival.

Eatonville town marker.

The Bernie Lee Trio performs at ZORA! Festival.

A variety of great food at the ZORA! Festival.

Traditional African dancers.

Storyteller Jackie Torrence

Anything We Love Can Be Saved:
The Resurrection of Zora Neale Hurston and Her Work

Alice Walker

Alice Walker is author of the novel The Color Purple, *winner of the National Book Award. Her other novels include* The Temple of My Familiar *and* Possessing the Secret of Joy. *Walker has also written collections of short stories, poetry, and essays. Her 1975 article "In Search of Zora Neale Hurston," published in* Ms *magazine, helped to revive interest in Hurston's work. Alice Walker was the keynote speaker at the first annual Zora Neale Hurston Festival of the Arts and Humanities in 1990.*

The First Annual Zora Neale Hurston Festival
Eatonville, Florida
January 26, 1990

My first visit to Eatonville was on August 15, 1973, seventeen years ago. I was 28, my daughter Rebecca, 3. Sometimes she tells me of the pain she felt in childhood because I was so often working, and not to be distracted, or off on some mysterious pilgrimage, the importance of which, next to herself, she could not understand. This trip to Eatonville, not one of whose living inhabitants I knew, represented such a pilgrimage, one that my small, necessarily stoic child would have to wait years to comprehend.

But at the time, I felt there was no alternative. I had read Robert Hememway's thoughtful and sensitive biography of Zora

Neale Hurston, after loving and teaching her work for a number of years, and I could not bear that she did not have a known grave. After all, with her pen she had erected a monument to the African-American and African-AmerIndian common people both she and I are descended from. After reading Hurston, anyone coming to the United States would know exactly where to go to find the remains of the culture that kept Southern black people going through centuries of white oppression. They could find what was left of the music; they could find what was left of the speech; they could find what was left of the dancing (I remember wanting to shout with joy to see that Zora, in one of her books, mentioned the "moochie," a dance that scandalized—and titillated--the elders in my community when I was a very small child, and that I had never seen mentioned anywhere); they could find what was left of the work, the people's relationship to the earth and to animals; they could find what was left of the orchards, the gardens and the fields; they could find what was left of the prayer.

I will never forget reading Zora, and seeing for the first time, written down, the prayer that my father, and all the old elders before him, prayed in church. The one that thanked God that the cover on his bed the night before was not his winding sheet, nor his bed itself his cooling board. When I read this prayer, I saw again the deeply sincere praying face of my father, and relived my own awareness of his passion, his gratitude for life, and his humbleness.

Nor will I forget finding a character in Zora's work called Shug. It is what my "outside" grandmother, my grandfather's lover and mother of two of my aunts, was called. It is also the nickname of an aunt, "Malsenior," for whom I was named. On any page in Zora's work I was likely to see something or someone I recognized; reading her tales of adventure and risk became an act of self-recognition and affirmation I'd experienced but rarely before.

Reading her, I saw, for the first time, my own specific culture, and recognized it as such, with its humor always striving to be equal to its pain, and I felt as if, indeed, I had been given a map that led to the remains of my literary country. The old country, as it were. Her characters spoke the language I'd heard th elders speaking all my life. Her work chronicled the behavior of the elders I'd witnessed. And she did not condescend to them, and she did not apologize for them, and she *was* them, delightedly.

It was very hot, my first visit to Eatonville. As hot in Florida as it had been in Jackson, Mississippi, where I lived, which I'd left early that morning, and where my small daughter remained, in the care of her father and her pre-school teacher, Mrs. Cornelius. I thought of her, as Charlotte Hunt and I drove about Eatonville and, later, Fort Pierce, on our mission. I wanted to mark Zora's grave, so that one day all our daughters and sons would be able to locate the remains of a human mountain in Florida's and America's so frequently flat terrain.

Today, knowing as I do the vanity of stones, their true impermanence, the pyramids notwithstanding, I would perhaps do things differently, but at the time my passionately held intention to erect a reminder of a heroic life indicated the best that I knew. And we were successful, I think, Charlotte Hunt and I, for we lifted the pall of embarrassment at our people's negligence off ourselves. We acted for Zora, yes, but in a way that relieved the shame of inactivity from ourselves. Paying homage to her, memorializing her light, her struggle and her end, brought us peace.

At least it brought me peace. I should perhaps not attempt to speak for Charlotte, who volunteered to be guide and companion to me. And yet I felt that Charlotte, too, loved Zora's spirit, and was no less concerned than I that her body not seem to have been thrown away.

But what is a dead body, what are bones, even of a loved one? If you mixed Zora's bones with those of Governor Bilbo's, for many years an especially racist oppressor of black people in

Mississippi and psychologically of the whole country, the untrained eye would not be able to tell them apart. And nature, in its wisdom, has made sure that the one thing required of all dead things is unfailingly met. That requirement is that they return to the earth, which in fact, even as living bodies, they have never left. It matters little, therefore, where our bodies finally lie, or how and whether their resting places are marked—I speak now of the dead, not of the living who have their own needs and project those onto the dead—for our ultimate end, blending with the matter of the earth, is inevitable and common. I hope, myself, to become ash that is mixed with the decomposing richness of my compost heap, that I may become flowers, trees and vegetables. It would please me to present the perfect mystery of myself, prior to being consumed by whomever, or whatever, as rutabaga or carrot. Sunflower or pecan tree. Eggplant.

The spirit, too, if we are lucky, is sometimes ground to ash by the trials of life and tossed on the collective soul's compost heap. That is what has happened to what we have come to know as Zora. That is why we are here today, honoring her; startled perhaps by the degree of nourishment each of us has gained from her, startling in our diversity.

Zora Hurston's ash was diamond ash.

Diamonds, you know, start out as carbon, or coal, deep in the folds of the earth. Over eons enormous pressure builds up and crushes the coal into diamonds, the hardest crystals known. Then some of us, like Zora, are crushed further, by the lies of enemies and the envious hostility of friends, by injustice, poverty and ill health, until all that is left is diamond ash. For many years now, thanks to Robert Hemenway, thanks to Mary Helen Washington, thanks to Charlotte Hunt, thanks to Sherley Anne Williams, thanks to feminist and womanist scholars around the world, and thanks to millions of readers, Zora's diamond ash, her spirit, has been blowing across the planet on the winds of our delight, our excitement, our love.

And this is only right; it is the universe's justice. And it proves something that I think many of us here very much needed to see proved, twenty-odd years ago, when the commonest comment about Zora was the question Zora Who?: that love and justice and truth are the only monuments that generate ever-widening circles of energy and life. Love and justice and truth the only monuments that endure, though trashed and trampled generation after generation. We have, together, accomplished the resurrection of Zora Neale Hurston and her splendid work, and can now tell our children what we have learned from this experience. Our children who are by now grown up enough to fly off on mysterious pilgrimages of their own. We can say with conviction that anything that they love can be sheltered by their love; anything they truly love can be saved. First in their own hearts, and then in the hearts of others. They have only to make their love inseparable from their belief.

We can tell them that on the day that we love ourselves, and believe we deserve our own love, we become as free as any earthbeings can ever be. And that we begin to see that, though our forms may differ, as an oak tree differs from a pine, we are in fact, the same. Zora is us. That is why, reading her, we smile or cry when she shows us our face.

I will close with this prayer which Zora collected, perhaps hoping that when black people read it, it would evoke for them one of the most longed for and truest images not only of the African-American face , but of the African-American psyche. For like all spiritually authentic peoples our ancestor understood that they did not need to be taught how to pray; that prayer, like poetry and music, of which it is mother, creates itself out of the lived experience, the pain and passion of the human heart. Typically, when poor black people sank to their knees, they created not a Lord's prayer, but a People's prayer.

I always weep when I read this, so bear with me.

". . . You have been with me from the earliest rocking of
my cradle up until this present moment,
You know our hearts, our Father,
And all de range of our deceitful minds.
And if you find anything like in lurking
In and around our hearts
Ah ast you, My Father, and my Wonder-workin' God
To pluck it out
And cast it into de sea of Fuhgitfulness
Where it will never rise to harm us in dis world
Nor condemn us in de judgment.
You heard me when Ah laid at hell's dark door
With no weapon in my hand
And no God in my heart,
And cried for three long days and nights.
You heard me, Lawd.
And stooped so low
And snatched me from the hell
Of eternal death and damnation.
You cut loose my stammerin' tongue;
You established my feet on de rock of salvation
And yo' voice was heard in rumblin' judgment.
I thank Thee that my last night's sleepin' couch
Was not my coolin' board
And my cover
Was not my windin' sheet.
Speak to de sinner-man and bless'im.
Touch all those
Who have been down to de doors of degradation.
Ketch de man dat's layin' in danger of consumin' fire;
And Lawd.
When Ah kin pray no mo';
When Ah done drunk down de last cup of sorrow
Look on me , yo' weak servant who feels de least of all;
'Point my soul a restin' place
Where Ah kin se down and praise yo' name forever
Is my prayer for Jesus sake
Amen and thank God.

Alice Walker

Folk art at the Outdoor Festival.

Dancers

Steel drummers

National Planner Dr. Richard A. Long

Traditional African drummers

Dolls in African clothing

A student plants a garden at Education Day.

A Conversation with Eatonville Elders:
Vera King, Frank M. Otey, and Ella Dinkins
Moderated by N.Y. Nathiri

This panel discussion was presented at the second annual Zora Neale Hurston Festival of the Arts and Humanities in 1991.

N.Y. Nathiri:

I want to start with Mrs. Vera King.

Mrs. Vera King:

I was born here. My mother was born here. My grandmother was born here in 1890—sorry, 1889—so we kinda go back quite a ways. I started first grade here and I finished here at the high school in twelfth grade, so it's home in more ways than one. The school has always been here as long as I can remember. The town has been here as long as I can remember, and that's been for sixty-three years, so it's home to me.

Mr. Otey:

Well mine's a long story, I suppose, but let's make it short. I was drafted off the college campus to come to Florida. I had heard of Florida, but never heard of Eatonville School. Principal came up and said he was looking for two or three teachers, and the dean sent for me, and we had a conference. I committed myself to come down here, and I came down.

You wouldn't believe it. I came in 1939. I graduated in college in '39. I came and stayed two-and-a-half years and went into the army, and when I left France into Germany, the war was over, and

I came back. At that time we moved to Indiana—I didn't come back down here. It was a boarding school, and one of the trustees sent me a wire saying, "We hear you are not in the service anymore. When are you coming back to work?" And I didn't answer. The next week he wired me and we talked. In fact he called and we talked, and I told him I had not planned to come back to Florida. I was going to grad school. He said, "No, you come back to Florida. We need you, and you can go to grad school in the summers and I'll pay all your expense." So that got my attention right quick. Since I had worked my way through college, somebody was going to give me money to go to grad school. So I came back, and I taught science, I taught physical education, and I ended up being dean of boys. Four years later I was asked to take over principalship. And I was here when this was built—almost everything you see here now was built under my administration.

And this young lady to my left was a student at that time. You would believe she worked as my secretary for about what, ten or twelve years, wasn't it? Yes. She worked as a secretary for ten or twelve years and left here and went to the Superintendent's office and worked as a supervisor for a while. I realized that I only had a couple of years and I could retire, so I asked to be transferred to one of the elementary schools. I took the school, and when the time came to retire, I left there and I have been a free bird ever since. That's in short a history part of my life here in Eatonville.

Mrs. Jenkins:

My first trip to Eatonville was [when] my father was a contracting builder and he built Mrs. Calhoun's home—it was a two-story brick house—and I fell off the Buick open door and broke my arm. That was in 1922. Then in 1930 we moved to Eatonville and we have been here ever since. There was a boarding school and I walked to school. [At] that time Captain Hall was our principal. Then, when I graduated from school in 1937, we had six students in our class, three boys and three girls. One boy—one young man is still living, and three of the girls are still living, so that's our class from 1935. I love this town. We knew everyone. When we moved here there were twenty-six houses and no electric lights, but we could tell every night when each family went to bed because they would blow the lamp light out. That was a great experience. You just have to learn to love where you live. I love this place.

N.Y. Nathiri:

Let me ask you this. What do you think is important for young people today who are in school? What are the kinds of lessons that you learned in school and that you wonder if these students are learning? Mr. Otey, will you start us off?

Mr. Otey:

Well, I sat here for the last five or six minutes looking over the crowd, trying to decide whether they were wondering too. I could tell by the blinking of the eyes and the and twisting of the heads. I think one of the first things you need to know is, you ought to have some desire, [some idea of] what you want to do in life, and then you need to find out how you can accomplish those desires, and what jobs you need to do, and what attitudes you need to develop, because you have to have a desire to be somebody, not your buddy, not your friend, but be somebody.

And in order to be somebody, you need to have a clean attitude. You look through the crowd and you say, "He's a pretty good guy, but he doesn't get his lessons, so I can't associate with him. She's a pretty good girl, but she hangs out, so I can't associate with her either." Once you decide what direction you want to go, you have to stick to it. You have a lot of bumps and knocks. Those of you who play ball, especially football, you realize you get a lot of hard knocks, but you have to take [them] when the time comes. Kids today young people today are too quick to give up. They want to hang out and stay home and miss school. But they can look around and see, how did he do so and so, and how did she do so and so. They had a desire and they worked toward it and I think that's what you need to have.

Unless you have an idea of what you want to do ten, fifteen, twenty years from now, you're spinning your wheels. And you need to open up and say, "I'm going to do this or I'm gonna do that." If you were to stop from here to home—and I don't know where you live—but if you were driving, the first thing you'd want to do is say, "Well, I'm going home. I'll go this way, then I make a right turn, and then make a left turn. Then I'll be home." You gotta know the roads. You gotta know the right roads, and if you don't know the right roads you gotta seek the right roads and pick them out and talk with people who are on the right road. And this is one of the things most of them don't have.

I watched a basketball game last night. How many of you watched the Magic last night? You find out on the Magic last night you had two stars playing against each other and one wanted to out-play the other, one wanted to out-shoot the other. The Magic star played hard but not hard enough, and Carter, who played for the other team, played a little harder. He made more baskets. But the Magic won the game. So in life you have to decide where you want to go and what you want to do and what you have to do in order to get there and when the hard knocks come take them and move on. That's enough. [Laughter.]

N.Y. Nathiri:

Would you like to add something to that before we go back to the history of the community?

Mrs. King:

No, I would like to say to the young people that the little bit you heard there, we heard quite a bit, and believe it or not, it stayed there. You remember a lot of things you were taught during high school if you would just listen and use it and be practical.

I would like to say to you young people that whatever courses you are in—for instance, I learned to type on a manual typewriter, and when we got the electric typewriter it was a privilege to type on it. But whatever you are exposed to, learn it

26

well, and I don't mean the bad things in your classes. You really need to try and learn it well because it will probably put you in the working world. You may move further, and what is good about it is that you can move further, but what you are exposed to now, learn it as well as you possibly can because it may just help you along the way, and you can move further along the way in doing what you want to do.

I know I may have strayed a little bit from it. I just wanted them to know that we had a lot of sessions that explained the facts of life and he didn't bite his tongue about it if it was necessary, and it was. All girls, that's what he did, he would drag all of us over to the chapel, and it's a situation where you didn't dare talk in there. It was very quiet in there. It's good, so just listen sometimes, and really use it to your advantage. Thank you.

N.Y. Nathiri:

Picking up on what Mrs. King was talking about, would you describe the classes that you took when you were at Hungerford?

Mrs. Jenkins:

Our classes were small classes, and our teachers were dedicated teachers, and one thing I want to say to you young people is, attitude is one of the most important things in life. When someone speaks to you, don't say "Mm-mm," but open your mouth and speak intelligent. And that means so much because children now, students now, don't want to say yes or no, or yes ma'am or no ma'am. They want to shrug their shoulders or give you a grunt. Attitude is very important.

N.Y. Nathiri:

A little bit about the classes that you took?

Mr. Otey:

Well, we had Algebra I and II, we had English, History, Geography, Hygiene, and of course we had a few sports, but not many.

N.Y. Nathiri:
Would you talk about the origin of Hungerford High School? How did Hungerford get started?

Mrs. King:
I have forgotten how many acres were donated by Mr. Hungerford. Robert Hungerford was his son for which the school was named. I'm trying to remember. Edward Hungerford was the father who donated the first hundred acres to be a school — I think somewhere along the line it said for colored children. They've taken that part out now, but it was put here in, I believe, 1889. I had a problem working out the exact date because I was really looking for some of the history.

There were other people who donated land and it ended up with quite a few acres of land. It has expanded — like I said, a lot of [what] is here now was not here at that time. A lot of it is memory of being out here and seeing it, but the purpose of it was to educate children. This is what it's all about and this is what's still going on.

They have improved on some of the buildings. The gym, for instance, was built in 1954. I was a junior, but through the years we have seen additions, and let me tell you there was some small places and some small classrooms. The lunch room even is twice the size now. In fact, when I first came out here it was down on another end of the campus. But [the school] has served and is still serving its purpose of [being] there to educate young folk, and that's basically what it was all about.

Ms. Jenkins:
I would like to add something to that. Hungerford was a sister school to Tuskegee Institute. All our teachers came from Tuskegee, Fisk, or Hampton when we was first here. Washington Carver came to our school and talked to us, and Booker T. Washington came here and talked to us.

We had different buildings for the girls and different buildings for the boys. In one girls' building, upstairs is where the girls stayed and downstairs was our kitchen and our dining area. Then we had Calhoun's hall, where we had our prayer service and the teachers lived upstairs.

This is a huge change from the time that I went here to school because all the buildings were wooden buildings. They did have one stone building. But it's just wonderful to see the change and see the teachers we had. How dedicated they were to the students. If you had trouble learning something, they took you aside and gave you the very foundation of what you needed to know, and that made a big difference with our children in school at that time.

N.Y. Nathiri:

I'd like to pick up on some of those names by a show of hands who recognizes the name. Fisk, Tuskegee—what was the other you mentioned?—Hampton, all right. George Washington Carver, Booker T. Washington. All right, now we are beginning to see Eatonville in a larger context. Some of you may know that Eatonville is properly known as the oldest incorporated African American municipality in the United States, and in fact the founder of Hungerford, the first principal, did come from Tuskegee Institute. So you see that marriage or that partnerships. Today we call them HBCUs, Historically Black Colleges, and the ones that she named come from what they call that first tier, Hampton, Fisk, Tuskegee—Hampton in Virginia, Tuskegee [in] Alabama, Fiske [in] Tennessee—Nashville, Tennessee.

Mr. Otey, how would you say what was the philosophy of education? In other words, as a leader here, what was your attitude toward the students' ability to learn? What were the standards that you expected from those students?

Mr. Otey:

Well one of my pet situations or sayings was, everybody learns. We didn't have any failures. At that time I could go in a classroom and just sit down, and that afternoon I would send for the teachers and we would have a talk. There's no sleeping in class—you sleep at home. There's no eating in class—you eat in the lunch room. We didn't do chewing gum in class. You decided what you want to do in life. And it worked out quite well. We had boys who were the valedictorians, we had girls who were valedictorians, salutatorians, and class leaders.

Our classes were so organized that each class had its own officers, and if there was somebody in the class goofing off—I don't know what you call [goofing off] today—but if they were out of line, the president of the class would say so. He stand and say, "Mr. So-and-So, Johnny, back here playing and not getting his work." And this wasn't a matter of being popular with the guy or the guy wouldn't like you. You told the truth, and it worked out.

We had a set curriculum. We had four English [classes], we had two maths, two sciences—or three sciences, really. We had the health, physical education, social studies. As I said earlier, I taught biology I and II, chemistry, general science, and the last [class] in the afternoon—I taught physical ed, coached basketball, football, and track. One teacher couldn't do that now. One teacher *wouldn't* do that now. [*Laughter.*] One teacher wouldn't train or teach themselves so they would be in a position to do that. I did that one year, but the next year I had a little conference room. Hey, let's divide this up. And it was divided and it worked out quite well.

Before they built all these high schools that you people go to, we had a bus [that] came from Tangerine, Plymouth, Apopka, and Winter Garden. Well, Winter Garden went into Orlando. Now these came over here, and Winter Park came over here, all of Winter Park. We had a conglomerate—we had kids coming from all over. And they had different ideas, but they had the chance to express their ideas, and we mold them into what we wanted them to be. We turned out doctors, lawyers, undertakers, teachers, whatever you wanted to name. We had scholarships offered to them from other places, and they did quite well. Tuskegee turned out a lot of them, A&M, Hampton, Howard University, and of course this was before your time, when they integrated. You go where ever you want. Then they started going wherever they wanted, and they did quite well, and they still are doing quite well.

So I think that's basically what [students] need to do. Once they get an idea of what they want to be and do, [if they] stick to it, they'll do quite well.

N.Y. Nathiri:

Let me break this for a little bit and ask if you have any comment or question about anything that you have heard at this point.

Let me repeat the question so you can all hear it. You are asking him or the panel to describe the length of the school day? Length of school day and how long was each period?

Mr. Otey:

Eight-thirty till three, and at that time every student had one planning period, one break. Had a planning period every day, and it was scheduled so he could spend the time mostly in the library. And it worked out pretty well.

Now, there were some smart ones who wouldn't want a planning period—they wanted an extra class, and we let them do that. So, instead of having two maths, he would have three maths—he takes algebra or geometry. That was special classes and special students. Does that answer your question? All right.

Youth Attendee:

Did you ever feel like you wanted to go see more of the world, being such a small community? Did you want to meet outsiders a lot?

Mrs. King:

You referring to me?

Yes, traveling is something I have not had a chance to do extensively. I ended up back [here] during my high school years. I lived in Winter Park, but we were bussed here. I was getting ready to go, I was working out here at the school, and my husband was drafted and going to Ohio, and of course he was drafted back into the service. And that kind of blew that, and I always fussed about how you're not supposed to be born, live, and die in the same place. But here I am.N.Y. Nathiri:

Let's talk about Eatonville in the 1920s and '30s, what it was actually like here, and we'll bring it up by decades. What kinds of changes occurred? Mrs. King and Mrs. Jenkins, can you talk about the Eatonville that you knew in the '20s and '30s?

Mrs. King:

In the '20s and '30s every family knew each other, and when you had a problem it was the families' problem, not just my problem. The community came together. If you needed a well dug, the men would go out and work all day long in the fields, but at night they would come and dig your well for you. They would build a fire so they could see how to put the pipes down, and when the water came they would say, "Oh, we got water," and then fix the pump and everyone would go home. Of course we always had food for them to eat while they were working at night like that. If children were naughty in the streets, you got chastised by your neighbors, and when you got home you got chastised again, but you got more chastisement [at home] than you did from the people outside.

This is the way it was. Yes ma'am, I can see you rolling your eyes. Our children were trained by our community along with the training they received at home, and that is why I must say we had better children then. We had naughty children, of course, but we didn't have the same things going on as you have going on now with children.

N.Y. Nathiri:
Okay.

Mrs Jenkins:
I forgot the question. *[Laughter.]*

N.Y. Nathiri:
Life in the twenties and thirties.

Mr. Otey:
Twenties and thirties? You weren't here.

Mrs. Jenkins:
I was going to say I just got here in thirty-seven.

N.Y. Nathiri:
Thirties and forties.

Mrs. King:
One of the things I remember—and I lived right down the street from the school—is the bell. I know you all have seen the bell on the campus. The bell was like a clock. It rang at a certain time in the morning. I think it meant that the students had to get up and do their chores. Then it would ring again, and they had breakfast, and then the third time was for them going to class. But that bell has always been a thing I remember.

Another thing I remember out here when I was small, I remember two street lights. One was by St. Lawrence, which is the oldest church, and the other was right across the street from the school. Those are the only two I remember. Kennedy Avenue was the only—what they called a hard road. If I remember correctly, it was so narrow they had to partially get off the road to pass. But those are a few of the things I remember. It's just a remarkable experience.

I remember neighbors sitting on your porch at night, and some of those grandmothers would tell stories that you would have nightmares about. You'd be afraid to go to bed. But [the stories were] also interesting and [the grandmothers] had a knack of doing a story on the spur of the moment and make it up as they go. Of course at that time, we didn't realize this was going on, but it was a unity kind of thing, that you knew your neighbors. You know the expression that it takes a whole village to raise a child. Well, if you lived out here, the village did.

I remember that through the years this particular school has always been a community school, in that if there was an activity going on here, you didn't have to have kids, but most of the people who lived in Eatonville, no matter what time we had an activity--a baccalaureate was eight o'clock in the morning—they came. And then they would go to their particular churches. If there was a game, they were here—in the gym when we did get a gym, even when we played basketball out behind the campus on a clay court—and that's an experience, believe me. I didn't play, but I used to attend the games.

I remember the streets being unpaved. It used to rain in the summer time a lot—practically every afternoon you could depend on it raining—and there were some streets you could not go down when it had rained like that because it was so muddy and your car would get stuck. I have seen through the years the sewage put in. We've gone from the outdoor toilet to the inside, and the elaborate stuff now. It's just so many changes, the sewage system, the water system, the street light—all of those things I have seen progress through the years. It's something to make you very proud of.

It's the same way I feel about the school. It has gone through a lot of changes. I'm getting away from Eatonville, but when I say that it's because the school is a part of Eatonville. You'll find in the history that its just as much a part of Eatonville as town hall, probably before they had a town hall, but it's all integrated together as a whole. It makes a whole with the school.

Mrs. Jenkins:
I would like to say something about the road out there. It was initially called Apopka, the old highway from 17-92 to Apopka. This was the only road they had to travel between the two communities. That road is about 150 years old now and has had three or four different names, from old Apopka Road to Eatonville Road to Lake Avenue to Kennedy Boulevard. I've seen all those changes in the road. As Mrs. King said, it was a narrow road and at one time it was not hard rocked, it was clear rocked down, and

she spoke about the cars getting stuck. And the clay would get on your cars and be muddy red. Zora always spoke about the road.

This small town at first was called a village because maybe fifty or a hundred people [lived] here. It's so interesting to see how many changes have come about [as] this small village [has grown] to a town.

N.Y. Nathiri:

Now there's about 3500 people here, so it's still a small town. Let's talk about Zora Neale Hurston as a person. Who here knew Zora Neal Hurston or met Zora Neale Hurston?

Mrs. Jenkins:

I knew Zora when I was a child, when she would do her writing. One day she took us to a place over in Casselberry called Lake Ferry. She had some friends out there, and it was on a lake where she could be quiet and do her writing. She carried us out there one day to do that, and then she would visit my mother in our home. She didn't come often, but when she did come she would always visit. She was a lovely person, just an ordinary person, she wasn't a person that looked over you, but she was a down-to-earth person. That's the kind of person she was.

N.Y. Nathiri:

Can you say how was it that you interacted with her, as your being a child?

Mrs. Jenkins:

Well, I don't know how to say this and I don't want to say it in the wrong wording, but we were interested in what she was doing with her writing, and she spoke about us in one of her books—the Johnson girls—so she would take us with her.

N.Y. Nathiri:

When you say "us," who would she take?

Mrs. Jenkins:

There were three older girls—my older sister, myself, and a sister under me—and my younger sister, Sadie. She was a small child, so [Zora] didn't take her really. We were called "young missy girls" at that time.

N.Y. Nathiri:

So when you say "young missy girls," that would be about what age?

Mrs. Jenkins:

Ten, twelve, fourteen.

N.Y. Nathiri:

I understand that Zora Neale Hurston used to take children out of Eatonville and put them in plays or skits. Do you know anything about that personally, either you or Mrs. King?

Mrs. King:

I had a few cousins who I heard say that they were in her plays when they went to Rollins. They would go over and perform. But I've never talked to them extensively about it.

Mr. Otey:

I met her twice. I think the first year I was down here, she was here, and I had a chance to talk to her. She was just another lady to me. I was just out of college. I had a few conversations [with her] and moved on. [Some] years later, she came back here. At that time I had just come back from the service, and this being a boarding school just like Rollins and other places, it meant we were here and we didn't have to go all over town and places. I had conversations with her several times, and she gave a performance at Rollins and persuaded four or five of us to go along so she would have some help with the audience. She gave a very good performance there.

I wrote the history of Eatonville, a hundred-year history of Eatonville, and I had a chance to do a lot of research. I went back to 1885 and we picked up the beginnings and moved on into the centennial, which was held in what, 1976 or '78?

Mrs. King:

Eighty-seven.

Mr. Otey:

Yeah, the centennial. The book gives account of the whole trip, the number of mayors, number of stores that were in town and what they did, and some of the outstanding people, the naming of streets, the expansion of the town itself. So it has quite bit of information that give you background of it. Those who graduated went to college and other towns and have other desires, and many of them don't come back. Some of them move on to other places, and they go [to] higher education, post [graduate] degrees.

Eatonville has doubled since I have been in this area. I have seen a lot of things happen, good and bad like all other towns, and it would be to your advantage if you could just know the history of it, and you make a decision of what are the good things and what are the things you would like to do in your life. What contributions can you make to your community and how hard must you work to make sure that it is a good contribution. Eatonville has had some people that have made good contributions and some that were has-beens, and you find those every place you go. That's probably enough.

Youth Attendee:

With all the changes that Eatonville has encountered, do you think the town has lost the richness and the [quality of] "it takes a village to raise a child"?

N.Y. Nathiri:

Did everyone hear the question?

Mr. Otey:

No, I couldn't either.

N.Y. Nathiri:

With all of the changes that Eatonville has endured, do you think that some of the richness of the community has been lost?

Mr. Otey:

I think that most of the changes have been for the good. If you had a chance to look back fifty-sixty years ago in some of the books and pictures and see the environment, the type of houses they had, and see what you see now, you would say to yourself, "Well, yeah, it was a good move." So they have added on and [had] good growth here in Eatonville. We have had some good leadership, and there is room for more.

Youth Attendee:

In some of Zora's books, critics say that she didn't address any racial tension that was in Eatonville or Florida at the time. Do you think there was any or that she portrayed it correctly?

Mr. Otey:

Well during my tour there was very little, because Eatonville was dubbed the bed town. People go to work in other places and come home and go to bed. They slept here but they worked in other places. A lot of them worked in Winter Park, and that's how Maitland grew because they lived here and worked in Maitland. There was a relationship that was developed between the people and the people they worked for, as now there's a pretty good relationship with the people you work for, so that's what you needed in racial tension.

N.Y. Nathiri:

You must remember that you wouldn't expect any racial tension in Eatonville. You might expect other kinds tensions. The reason I'm saying that is because everybody in Eatonville was all the same race. As a matter of fact, I believe she says in *Dust Tracks on the Road* that in Eatonville you got what you brought. In other words there were no artificial distinctions or any excuses. Whatever you were, people recognized you for those qualities because you couldn't decide, "Oh, she's black, and that's why she does that," or "That's a black thing," or things like that because everyone in Eatonville was of African-American heritage. So in that sense Eatonville was like an incubator. You knew who you were and you could assess people's character without having to worry about the lens of race. Of course, outside of Eatonville there might be other circumstances.

Youth Attendee:
Were there still prejudices against financial situations or other types of situations?

N.Y. Nathiri:
Yes. I would make some comment just in terms of my having grown up here in the 1950s and '60s. I think you raise a good issue. I think that in all communities there is classism, there is social status. People who are working in certain areas might be seen in a certain light because of their employment. So I think that certainly could and did exist. But I'll ask the others. Mrs. King?

Mrs. King:
It exists now, but I was thinking back and basically most of the people who lived here were kinda on the same level. I really don't think [social status] came into play too often. By the time I got into high school, things had changed--people were doing different things—but [in] a small town. I really don't think it was that much different. It was not a "I-got-a-whole-lot-and-you-don't-have-very-much" kind of a thing. I am just used to [people] sharing, and this is basically what they did during my time as a youngster. I can remember that, and I don't ever remember feeling the kind of things that you all go through now, of feeling that you maybe are "above" or "below" and that kind of thing. I just don't remember encountering that. Like I said, now it's a horse of a different color. It's different.

Mrs Jenkins:

Well, when I was a child everyone lived together in harmony. There was no "I'm better than you" or "You worse than I am." We just all lived like a family. Eatonville when I came here was a family home. We all lived together and we shared together. If you grew up [on a] farm and I had something in my garden that you didn't have in your garden, we gave you some of what we had. If you killed a hog or a cow, we all shared that together. We were all family. It wasn't like it is now. You live in Casselberry and your home is a better home than what I have. We all lived on the same level.

Youth attendee:

What in your opinion brought about the change from being a family-type community, where everyone shared, to a more divided community, more like the rest of the world?

Mrs. Jenkins:

Well, the war [World War II] made a big difference in the whole world because the people then had made more money and they got different subdivisions and different areas to live in. If you lived in a two-bedroom home and you made a little bit more money, then you were going to leave that two-bedroom home and go to a four-bedroom home. Then, if you lived on a lake and you thought, "Ooh, I'm living on a lake, now I need a two-story with a pool and all the things that go with it." So that is what made the difference really, finances.

Mrs. King:

I think, too, a lot of the people who lived along that level that I was talking about are all gone. There was a time when we knew everybody here and now you don't. Most of the people who live out here I don't know. Most of them have moved in from other communities. There are still a few, [but] you will find very few natives out here, people who were born here. Most of them have died off. I think that helped to make a difference in how [people here] feel, whether being "up" or "down." But we do have a lot of people who came from other places, like they do everywhere. When it started out, families knew each other and they just kinda stuck together. Whether "you need" or "I need," we helped each other.

Mr. Otey:

Well, over a hundred years there are changes, over thirty years there are changes, over twenty years there are changes. Most of your parents, if you lived in Orlando, went to one of three or four schools, Colonial, Edgewater, Boone, or Winter Park High School. Now the high schools have doubled and tripled and you are spread out all over. And we had a little old track team, so this was the center point, and everybody came to see what was going on. And churches were in walking distance. Everyone went to one of the three churches here. So you had a togetherness of a lot of things. You didn't have all this separatism that we have now, all those out-doing each other or out-smarting each other. You didn't have all that and it worked out.

I had a boy I was talking to just last week. He liked to cut class. At nine o'clock each morning all the teachers sent their attendance slips to my [office] and I looked through [them] to see who was absent and who wasn't, and if I recognized a name on the list—sometimes there would be two or three of them—at nine-thirty I'd go down to Winter Park and go through the square and come back around, and sometimes I catch them right there. I wouldn't bring them back to school. I'd give them till ten o'clock to meet me back here, to come to my office, and then we had some discipline problems. Don't think everything was rosy. When I came [here] this place was covered with oak trees, a lot of oak and pine trees through here, and out there where they played ball and stuff was almost a wilderness. The biggest discipline problem we had, they had a choice of three days at home with the momma bringing them back on the third day—or the father, whichever, it didn't matter—or he could dig one of the trees with a stump on it, and that was the hard one, but they'd do it and boast the fact that "Yes, I did it, I did it." So there were a lot of little things that made the thing work. The young ladies who kinda goofed off a little bit—the circle right out here in the front was much larger—they'd either streak the circle or make fifty laps around the circle, just walk around it fifty times. And you could sit and look out the window and count 'em if you wanted, or I would get the chairman of one the classes to sit out here and count the laps So-and-So'd take. The student council was pretty strong, so they controlled that and we didn't have any discipline problems.

And you'd be surprised, 95 percent of the kids who came into the seventh grade—we had seventh through twelfth—if their parents didn't move out of town, they graduated. We didn't have any fall-outs and misses and flunks and stuff like that. We didn't have that because PTA met every month, mothers or fathers came, both of them came most of the time, and if they didn't we'd look around, take roll. Next day the teachers would tell me that So-and-So didn't have anybody here representing them.

So I'd get in touch with the mother and say, "You didn't come to PTA last week" or "last month."

"Well, I was busy with so-and-so."

"Well, you missed something. Don't you miss the next one."

And she'd come. I could tell her that Johnny cut class twice or Mary was getting low grades, and we just talk like we are talking now. And the mother would get them home and tell them what's going on here, and that took care of it.

Youth attendee:

How important do you think was religion was to the community?

Mr. Otey:

Very, very strong. That is why it took the three agencies to run the town, the school, the churches and the city itself, because on the city council there were always one or two teachers and there were two or three either deacons or trustees from the churches, so there was a togetherness. You don't have that now, but that's what used to be. That kept down a lot of the discipline, and then the mothers and fathers had to work, and they didn't have time for the kids to be fooling around, wasting their money or time and skipping school. These kids are getting restless.

N.Y. Nathiri:
Dr. Ward?

Dr. Ward:
There is one question I want to raise about some of the representation of Eatonville, because I think it might become problematic for us as readers of the book *Their Eyes Were Watching God*. She doesn't exactly contemplate anything that the elders of the community had said. On the other hand, there is a strength in something that I think is the spirit and harmony of this place, and it was called "who talked about who." I go back to Janie's return as it is given here, and the people looking at her coming down the road say, "Where's the dress you left here with and what happened to the money? Of course, what happened to this young sister that went off? I bet he thought he was talking with another woman because she is an old woman now, trying to walk like she is young with her hair hanging down her back." You know that is a part of the history of small towns and I'd like for you to say a few things about the gossip that went on in Eatonville.

Mr. Otey:
Maybe I could help you a little bit, since I did a research for a whole hundred years. There has always been gossip in all towns and Eatonville was no different from the other towns. But it was small gossip, and some people didn't get it and some people did, so those people who did had some select places that they did this gossip. Down on the left, diagonally across from the club, there was a two-story building, and right next to it was a store, and you might read where she gave an account of the gossip that went on in the store, or on the porch of the store. Now, when I was doing the research, there were some people who passed on now but they were in their seventies and eighties. They verified it, it was true, they did that. Sometimes they'd talk about So-and-So in the

churches—at this little place, the store, they would sit out on the porch, they'd gossip about So-and-So, and they would see him coming and would get quiet about it until he left, and then they'd talk about it some more.

Zora talked about it in several of her books. *Dust Tracks on the Road,* I think you will find where she indicated something about the gossip. And she didn't get much publicity on it because the folks of Eatonville got to the place where they didn't like her. You didn't know that, did you?

Dr. Ward:

I had heard that.

Mr. Otey:

They said when she came to town, she dug up all the dirt she could find and then she would spread it out, laughing.

Dr. Ward:

I think what I said this morning, about the importance to speaking to the elders of any community, was very much confirmed by this wonderful panel discussion, I want to thank all the members of this panel for doing this for us.

Ella Dinkins

Singer Peabo Bryson

Artist Arthur Rayford

Young performers

National Planner Carrie Mae Weems

Women of Zeta Phi Beta sorority sponsor Education Day activities.

HATtitude Luncheon

Sheldon Hackney (right) chairman of the National Endowment for the Humanities.

Remembering the Life and Times of Zora Neale Hurston: Winifred Hurston Clark, Evelyn Hester, Ella Dinkins, and Babe Brown

Moderated by N.Y. Nathiri

This panel discussion was presented at the fifth annual Zora Neale Hurston Festival of the Arts and Humanities in 1994.

N.Y. Nathiri:

We are very grateful to have in our presence this group of seniors, the youngest of whom is 75 years old. All of these people have known Zora Neale Hurston in the flesh, and so we thought it would be [a] very interesting evening to have them recollect their remembrances of [her]. I am going to ask that each of them start off by saying something about the Zora Neale Hurston that they knew, [and] the circumstances under which they knew Zora. It's fitting, of course, that we start with family, and with Mrs. Winifred Hurston Clark, her oldest living niece.

Mrs. Winifred Hurston Clark:

I always think about Zora when I was small. She used to come to Memphis to visit us, and she [would] never tell us when, but she would just show up and we would be so happy to have her. Our community was very small and everybody knew everybody, and as soon as she came to town the kids—especially in the family—would tell everybody she was there, and they would call up Miss Zora. Most of them would call her Miss Zora and refer to her as dark sister.

She wore flashy beautiful clothes, and once she wore pajamas. At that time women didn't go in the street in pajamas, and she had some beautiful flower pajamas. I'll never forget it. She was on the street, going to neighbors and visiting in [her pajamas]. I had a friend—Alice, her name was—Alice Dempson. We were very, very close friends. She was crazy about our Zora. She would stay at our house most of the time [when Zora] was there. One day she came there [when] Zora had the pretty pajamas on, and the next day [Alice] wore some sleeping pajamas. They were pretty, but they were sleeping pajamas. She wore them to one of the neighborhood grocers, and the man in there told her, "You can't do like Zora." She said it hurt her feelings so bad, she went home and took them off.

After I got grown and finished high school, I lived with Aunt Zora for about eleven months. I enjoyed living with her. At times, when she was working on her writing or anything, she would go out under on a lake right across from Ms. Jenkins. That's where I learned to swim, when I came to Florida—right there in that lake. She would entertain us when she had her spare time, but at times when she was working she would go out under the tree and sometimes stay for hours and hours and hours. We didn't bother her—we knew not to bother her then. When she had time, she would come in and we would all laugh and talk. She was very nice to everybody.

N.Y. Nathiri:
Evelyn Hester was the daughter of Mathilda Mosley. In some writings Zora Neale Hurston makes reference to Mathilda Mosley, so you [are] here as the daughter of her best friend. Could you tell us a little bit about your reminiscence of Zora [when you were] a child?

Evelyn Hester:

Yes, it's just like her niece said, you never knew where Zora was. She would be, say, six months here, and she would disappear. You never knew when she left, and all of a sudden you would hear a knock at the door and it's Zora. She says, "Timmy, I'm here." She never says where she went or where she's going or nothing.

She had [a] show, and of course I had to be in it, as my mama tells me, "You do what Zora wants you to do." We did our rehearsals up here on 17-92, where Maitland's boat dock is now. It was [the] Johnson's house. We did all the dyeing of the cork stoppers. In those days you got your wine and your beer, but you could buy a big bag of cork stoppers. I guess some people in here know what that is. We did all colors, and we strung them to wear around our necks and ankles. And we did all the grass skirts [but] we didn't have grass. We used that heavy raffia that we used to do in school back in the days. We dyed all the colors we didn't have, and then made our hip skirts. I was a dancer. You wouldn't believe it now, but we played at Rollins College, and then we went down to Mountain Lake at this big golf club, and we had a wonderful time going down. We had about ten flat tires, no food, no water, and in those days you couldn't go to the bathroom. You had to just ride on until you [could] go to the woods. When we got to the Mountain Lake, we were starved but we had to do our show before we ate because we were late getting there. After the show they let us in the kitchen and we ate, and I'm telling you we had to get some of those boys out—we just had to drag them out, they were eating so much. I think they tried to eat [our hosts] out of house and home. *[Laughter.]*

It was all a wonderful time we had with Zora, and I never heard her say one bad word about anybody. It was always a smile, and [with that smile] she could get you to do anything she wanted you to do. She'd look at you and you'd go right on behind her, do anything. So that's my part of Zora.

N.Y. Nathiri

Ella Dinkins, Zora Neale Hurston was a college graduate. Your mother was a college graduate. Did you see any of the same signs of Zora as your two couch mates [saw], or did you see other elements that you could add to her description of her character?

Ella Dinkins:

Well, I can remember when Zora would come to our house, my mother and Zora would sit together and they would talk about Atlanta University and Dr. Dubois. The literary world is what they would talk about, and it was very enjoyable. We always had to sit very quiet and listen to whatever Zora had to say because she was very uplifting to hear.

N.Y. Nathiri

Can you tell us a little bit more? When you say "uplifting," do you remember things in particular? When you say "the literary [world]," how did you know it was books she was talking about?

Ella Dinkins:

She talked about Paul Laurence Dunbar, and I was going to school. We learned about Paul Laurence Dunbar and his [poetry]. She would talk a little bit about Langston Hughes, just a little bit, but he wasn't as well known as Paul Laurence Dunbar to us.

N.Y. Nathiri

All right. Mr. Brown, I believe you also were in Zora's plays, were you not? Could you tell us how you first came to know her, and some of the productions you were in, and your acquaintanceship with her?

Mr. Brown:

I met Zora in Winter Park, and she was looking for actors and singers, and someone had told [her] about me. At that time I was singing with the Down in Dixie Quartet and I was also singing in the Bethel Jubilee choir. We were very famous, so Zora came to me and said, "Sing, brother," and I did. She didn't have the songs that was popular that day. She had us to sing old white songs and "Working on the Railroad" and gambling songs that we made famous—"Let the deal go down, boy," and we'd throw the cards out, but the pastor got in us about that. We made those songs famous.

Zora had lots of white friends, and we would go to the white people's homes and sing for them, and they would give us plenty to eat. Then we begin to go to Rollins College. We gave a play at Rollins College—a play that Zora made up in, I guess, about thirty minutes. She say, "No, you start it off like that, buh buh buh." [In one of our plays we had a man] that could whistle like any bird. She told him, "You do that and you do this," so he got up there and asked people, "What kind of bird you want me to whistle?" They would tell him, and he'd whistle like the birds. So he became very famous, and he came back rich, just [from] whistling like birds.

We went to the folk festival in Washington, D.C. We made a big hit up there with singing different songs. Instead of the old Negro spiritual, we were singing white songs. We had sticks in our hands like black people working on the railroad and one of the verses would say, "When I get in Illinois, I'm gonna tell you all about the Florida boys," and then we would pull that stick up like we were moving the railroad. So we did fine up north.

Let me see, another place we went was some of the hotels around, so we became kinda famous until at one time our heads had to use the actors here. We supposed to be in New York.

We had lots of fun with Zora. Just to see how she could make up a play in about ten or fifteen minutes is unbelievable. That's the way we got it off. We had a very fine time and she was a very nice lady.

N.Y. Nathiri:
Now, about how old were you at this time? I'm interested in the people who were in the plays. Particularly, how old a young man where you when you were in Zora Neale Huston's plays?

Mr. Brown:
I guess about fifteen years old, fifteen or sixteen, something like that.

N.Y. Nathiri:
About fifteen?
How about you, Miss Evelyn?

Evelyn Hester:
About fourteen going on fifteen.

N.Y. Nathiri:
About fourteen?
Now, let me ask you this. Because we know not all was sweetness and light with Zora Neale Hurston in Eatonville, can you talk a little bit about how people in Eatonville perceived or how they thought about Zora Neale Hurston and what she was doing with the plays?

Evelyn Hester:
Are you speaking to me?

N.Y. Nathiri:
To both you and Ms. Ella Dinkins, but you first.

Evelyn Hester:
Well, the people of Eatonville didn't really think very much of her plays because she used—as he was saying—the old railroad cross ties songs. They had worked in it so long till they didn't want to hear it. They [said], "Well, if I got to go and see a show, I don't want to see [one] about what I have been doing all day long, you know?" But where other people liked it, they didn't, and quite a few didn't like her books for the same reason. It [was] as if they were trying to get away from all that kind of stuff she was writing about, and they just didn't like it.

N.Y. Nathiri:
Do you want to add anything to that, Mrs. Dinkins?

Ella Dinkins:
Well, Zora wrote it as it was. She wrote life just as it was. I can remember. My sister was relating to me today that we owned some land in Eatonville, and she said Zora said, "This much land, you should build

motels out here. Say, it would be a great thing for Eatonville to have motels." Zora thought about things way ahead of time. Who would have thought about a motel in Eatonville but Zora Neale Hurston years back? Now we do have one, but she thought about this fifty years ago, about the progress that Eatonville could make.

N.Y. Nathiri:

Now, when you were living [with] her, Miss Winifred—I have seen pages of writing where she has corresponded with you, and you were what, seventeen or eighteen when you lived with Zora Neal Hurston?

Mrs. Winifred Hurston Clark:

Yes, that's about right. Yes, about eighteen. Well, I finished high school, I was about eighteen.

N.Y. Nathiri:

About eighteen? Could you tell us a little? You've talked a little bit about her work habits. Did you know that she was a writer, a famous writer?

Mrs. Winifred Hurston Clark:

Yes, I knew she was a famous writer, but as time went on it was more talk about her. At that time it wasn't too much talking about her, but as time went on, just like now, she is very famous everywhere. Everybody talked about her [then], everybody talks about her books and everything [now], and [in] these black history programs, most time someone brings her up. I know in our church in Memphis they had black writers and photos of her, and she had me on [a] program talking about Zora. So as time went on she was very [much] thought of [as she is] now.

N.Y. Nathiri:

Did she talk to any of you about why she was doing the plays? In other words, you've talked about the fact that she could do them very quickly. Ms. Hester, you've said that you didn't have a script. Talk to us a little bit about how those plays went.

Evelyn Hester:

Well, she would say, "All right, on stage," and we would all line up on stage, and she stand here and [say,] "You do this, and you dance, and you don't know what dance you gonna do, just do something, just dance, and I'll tell you if it's not what [I] want." She would show you what she wants, but no script. I don't know how she did it, but that's the way it was done.

N.Y. Nathiri:

Did she talk to you about the underlying meaning, or why she was trying to organize it this way so you might get a better idea what you needed to do?

Evelyn Hester:

No. No, as I say, you knew nothing, you did what she said, and that's it, and I was one of them.

N.Y. Nathiri:

Well, you tell me about your costumes. How did you get your costumes?

Evelyn Hester:

Now, she she got all the paraphernalia for the costumes like the bags [and] cork stoppers, all different sizes, and this raffia came in a big bottle, and the corn, and we had to tie this raffia on corn, measure around your waist. And we took the big needles and ran the thread through after we dyed the cork stoppers, and then we made the anklets for your ankles, and we made the necklace for your necklace, and we did all of that for your arms and for your everything.

It was like [a] Hawaiian dress. Can you imagine me now, back in those days, in a Hawaiian dress? And we danced — I was in the chorus line.

N.Y. Nathiri:

Now we know that in the late 1940s Zora Neale Hurston had some real adversity. Did you all hear about the case that was in the newspapers, I think it was in New York when she was arrested and indicted on those felony charges? Did you hear anything about that?

Evelyn Hester:
No, we—I didn't.

Mrs. Winifred Hurston Clark:
No, I didn't either.

N.Y. Nathiri:
Are there any people who have questions that you might want to ask that might help us, as we are trying to recreate what was the persona of Zora Neale Hurston? Any questions?

Attendee:
There is some controversy of what was Zora's actual age. Some people say she was actually ten years older than she claimed to be in public. Do you know if this is a fact? And, if it is true, do you know at what time in her life she decided to take ten years off?

N.Y. Nathiri:
The family records show she was born in 1891, not 1901.

Mrs. Winifred Hurston Clark:
I have the record.

N.Y. Nathiri:
Do you want to talk a little bit about that, Miss Winifred?

Mrs. Winifred Hurston Clark:
I know that when Zora did put her age, she claimed to be younger, but she wasn't as young as she claimed, because I have an old family record with each of thems age on it, Zora's mother and all the kids. [Zora] was born in—I think what you said, 1891—yeah, because Matilda Mosley and Zora Neale Hurston was the same age.

Evelyn Hester:

I wondered who said that.

Mrs. Winifred Hurston Clark:

And she was born in 1891.

N.Y. Nathiri:

And so was Addie Johnson.

Mrs. Winifred Hurston Clark:

And I know I heard my mother laugh once or twice about it. They weren't talking to me. I was a good listener when I wasn't supposed to [be listening]. But [when] I heard her say, "Zora put her age back," what was I supposed to do but listen?

Attendee:

Mrs. Clark, how did her brothers and sisters view her? What where her relations like with the brothers and sisters? Were they good or did they fight a lot?

Mrs. Winifred Hurston Clark:

No, as far as I know they were very proud of Zora. Now, my Uncle Everett, when I was living in Connecticut, I went to his apartment to visit, and he just had his walls covered with things about Zora. And my father, he was the oldest brother. He died in 1935, so he didn't know too much about her accomplishments, but as far as I know all of them were crazy about her, proud of her.

Attendee:

This question is for Miss Clark. I was wondering, when you were staying with her, was she working on any major novels or was she working on articles?

Mrs. Winifred Hurston Clark:

Really, I don't know what she was working on, because she would always be outside and she never discussed it when she came inside, and I really don't know if she was working on a novel or what.

Lucy Anne Hurston, Zora's niece

Artistic director Elizabeth Van Dyke (center) with the Hurston family.

Opera singer Etta Moten Barnett

African clothing for sale at the Outdoor Festival.

Bethune Cookman College Choir

Dance!

More dance!

Poet Sonia Sanchez

Zora, Women, Life, and Love:
A Conversation with Dr. Maya Angelou
and Dr. Eleanor Traylor

Poet and performing artist Maya Angelou has written more than two dozen award winning books including I Know Why the Caged Bird Sings, All God's Children Need Traveling Shoes, *and* Gather Together in My Name. *In January 1993, Angelou made history by reciting her poem "On the Pulse of the Morning" at the inauguration ceremony of President Bill Clinton. Eleanor Traylor is Graduate Professor of English at Howard University and an acclaimed scholar in African American literature and criticism. She has written numerous chapters and essays, biographies, articles, and papers on African American writers including James Baldwin, Toni Morrison, and Richard Wright. Dr. Angelou and Dr. Traylor spoke at the fifth annual* Zora Neale Hurston Festival of the Arts and Humanities in 1994.

Patricia Merritt Watson:

My brothers and sisters, good evening. I am Patricia Merritt Watson. It is my pleasure to welcome you to this gala event highlighted by a conversation between Dr. Maya Angelou and Dr. Eleanor Traylor. This Fifth Zora Neale Hurston Festival of the Arts and Humanities, with its global implications, has been one of the crown jewels in a celebration of a woman who celebrated life, love, independence, and the folk. The scholarship that has been disseminated over the past week brings to mind a quote from Zora: "If you can see the light at daybreak, you don't care if you die at dusk. There are so many people never seen the light at all." Would you please join us, Mr. Harry Burney accompanied by Mr. Bateman, in the rendering of "Lift Every Voice and Sing," the Negro national anthem. Please stand.

[Song: "Lift Every Voice and Sing"]

Patricia Merritt Watson:

Dr. Gary Whitehouse, provost and vice president of academic affairs here at the University of Central Florida, will extend a salutation. Dr. Whitehouse.

Dr. Gary Whitehouse:

On behalf of the University of Central Florida and our president, John Hitt, I would like to extend our warmest welcome to you today. We at the university are pleased to be participating in the week-long international celebration of Zora Neale Hurston's life and works. In that spirit I would like to invite you back to the University of Central Florida campus, to our UCF gallery where we have a special exhibit by Betye Saar entitled "Sanctified Visions," which will be here until February 28. Zora Neale Hurston, the Eatonville writer, folklorist, and anthropologist, might have faded away into obscurity were it not for the work of a few dedicated scholars and the subsequent community efforts like this festival. Today Zora is recognized as a major contributor to the twentieth century literature, a preeminent African-American author, an inspiration to scores of writers and artists who have followed. We at UCF join you in celebrating the memory and contributions of Zora Neale Hurston, and we hope you enjoy this evening's program. Thank you.

Patricia Merritt Watson:

There has been a slight change in our program this evening. I am pleased to present two of the anchors who have planned and worked very hard to see that each festival is a little bit better than its predecessor. Mrs. N.Y. Nathiri and Mrs. Eddis Dexter, would you please come forward? These lovely ladies will host a brief award ceremony.

Eddis Dexter:

We want to thank all of you for being here today, and we want to say that for all of you who have helped us through this week and through the years, we realize we cannot call you individually, but we want all of you to know that we appreciate all that you have done for us. Our McKnight Achievers are working here tonight as our ushers and our hostess and all of our wonderful, wonderful volunteers. At this time we'd like to make some special presentations.

N.Y Nathiri:

On behalf of the Association to Preserve the Eatonville Community, Incorporated, we want to acknowledge those people who over the years worked to help to bring the Fifth Annual Zora Neale Hurston Festival of the Arts and Humanities into being. We want to acknowledge underwriters, local advisory council members, management team members, planners, and board members. Would you please hold your applause until after each category has been identified and asked to come forward?

In the fall of 1991, we presented the idea of the Fifth Annual Zora Neale Hurston Festival to the Central Florida community. There was a group of people who from the very beginning were in support of this, and I want to distinguish those members now of the local advisory council. Starting first with Mr. Bill McArthur and Mr. Herb Von Kluge of the Brooksville Development Corporation and the Orlando Plaza partners; Mr. Kessler from Atlanta of Kessler Enterprise; United Telephone of Florida, a Sprint Company; Mr. Donald Pointer; Walt Disney World Community Relations; Mr. Bob Wagner and Miss Patty DeYoung, representing the General Mills Restaurants Incorporated; Mr. Jeff Fuqua, chairman of the Greater Aviation Authority; the honorable Linda Chapin, Chairman of the Orange County Board of County Commissioners; the Florida Humanities Council; the City of

Orlando, led by the honorable Glenda H. Hood; the town of Eatonville, led by Mayor Harry Bing; the Florida Arts Council; Florida Department of State; and the Arts Services Council. Would those members who are present please stand and come forward? *[Applause.]*

Presented to all of you in appreciation for your outstanding service and personal commitment to the Fifth Annual Zora Neale Hurston Festival and International Celebration, January 24-30, 1994. Will you accept this award? We will give the individual plaques at the end of the awards.

A part of the brain trust for Hurston Festival '94 is an organization known as a local advisory council. These people have met on a quarterly interim basis to help move forward the financial resources needed for Festival '94. I would [like] to acknowledge each of them and ask them to come forward if they are present: Dr. Richard Astro; Mr. Darryl O'Benton; Congresswoman Corrine Brown; Miss Patti DeYoung; Mrs. Eddis Dexter; Miss Carolyn Fennell; Mr. George Fuller; Mr. Jeff Fuqua; Dr. George Grant; Mr. Luis Hughes; Mr. Alvin B. Jackson Jr.; Dr. Judith Cullver-Saars; Mr. Walter M. Koulash; Mr. Bill McArthur; Mr. Chris Miliotis; Miss Lisa Nason; Mr. William Nolan; Mr. Donald Pointer; Miss Sybil Pritchard; Representative Alzo J. Reddick; Mr. Johnny Rivers; Mr. Jay St. John; Dr. Thaddeus Seymour, the chairman of the local advisory council; Representative Bob Sindler; Dr. Shelia Smalley, representing the Zeta Phi Beta sorority Inc.; Mr. Herb Von Kluge; Mr. Bob Wagner; and Dr. Stephen Caldwell Wright. *[Applause.]*

If you will turn to the audience, no you needn't bow. *[Applause.]*

There is a group of people who actually get the work done. They are the management team members, the committee for juried art, the judges for the center stage performances, Mr. Ernest Manning, Mr. Walter Koulash, Mrs. Ernestine McWhite, Mrs. Yvonne Holt, Mrs. Juanita Sanders, Miss Tina Beecham, Miss Hortense Jones, Miss Gloria Lewis, Miss Jane Turner,

Councilwoman Louise Johnson Wright, Mr. Leon Theodore, Miss Maxine Hickson, Miss Katy Wright, Mrs. Adelaide Baldwin, Mr. Alton Lathrop, Mr. Carlton Whatley. Would you come forward please and be acknowledged? *[Applause.]*

Thank you very much. *[Applause.]*

Patricia Merritt Watson:

Dr. M. J. Hewitt of Santa Monica, California, president of Samjai Fine Arts, Incorporated, will present and introduce our illustrious guests for the evening.

Dr. M. J. Hewitt:

Good evening. . . . This [is] going to be a great evening, even though I have lost my notes, but that's okay, we don't need them. I think Zora Neale Hurston's spirit is here with us tonight, don't you? Yeah. One of the things I loved so much that she wrote was an explication about High John the Conquer. She said in that explication that those whom the gods would not destroy were armed with love and laughter. And that's what we are going [to] hear a lot about tonight, is love and laughter, love and laughter as creative survival, and that's what our two conversants are armed with. You already know from your program who Dr. Maya Angelou is and Dr. Eleanor Traylor. They are both my sister friends, and I am honored to be able to present them to you Dr. Maya Angelou and Dr. Eleanor Traylor. *[Applause.]*

Dr. Maya Angelou:

Ladies and gentlemen, brothers and sisters, family, this is an attempt to have a conversation in a three-walled room, so you are sitting as the third wall, listening to the conversation between two sister friends about a great African American woman and about a people.

Dr. Eleanor Traylor:

Sister.

Dr. Maya Angelou:
Sister.

Dr. Eleanor Traylor:
My beloved, if she had only known that this was her seventh dream, all of us who have come to her gatepost of the world, Eatonville, Maitland, Winter Park, Orlando, to her orange groves, to her pear trees.

She said that she had six dreams. Six were realized in her lifetime. The seventh she could only envision dimly. How could she envision you? How could she envision N. Y. Nathiri? How could she envision the committee to preserve historic Eatonville, which is now one of the most important regions on the literary map of the world? How could she envision the local advisory committee? How could she envision the princesses and princes of academe, of the business world, of the world of home and family, all coming here in her name? Most of all, how could she envision Maya Angelou who—

Dr. Maya Angelou:
Oh, Sister.

Dr. Eleanor Traylor:
Who inhabits the sun as though it were the only natural place to live. And finally, how could she envision a humble-born, south-Georgia-born little girl called Eleanor Traylor, who would be invited to assume a stage with Maya Angelou to speak about her? *[Laughter and applause.]*

Sister will not allow me to call all the names. I'm prepared to call all the names that we thank for this moment. I won't dare to—

Dr. Maya Angelou:
Thank you

Dr. Eleanor Traylor:
Because she will stop me. But please accept our thanks with all our hearts.

Dr. Maya Angelou:
Yes, when you're just getting a first brush of the stroke of genius that is Eleanor Traylor, you've got something coming to you.

Langston wrote "Note on Commercial Theatre," he said:, you have taken my blues and gone, you sing 'em on Broadway, and you fix them so they don't even sound like me, yes, you've taken my blues and gone. You also took my spirituals and gone, but someday somebody will stand up and talk about me and put on plays about me and write about me, black and beautiful, and sing about me and put on plays about me. I reckon it will be me myself, yes, it will be me.[1]

So it is wonderful and of more than passing interest that Miss Zora Neale Hurston said, "I will write about me." And she used the first person singular, "me, I, me, myself," to mean the first person plural, "we," so that when she spoke, she spoke in the same voice as Mr. Fredrick Douglass, which was always "I say I, I mean we." So I think it is in that voice that we hear her genius. Wouldn't you?

Dr. Eleanor Traylor:

Oh yes, yes, and her genius was so singular, so wonderful, so complete, but also so seemingly prepared for—

Dr. Maya Angelou:

Yeah.

Dr. Eleanor Traylor:

A tradition behind her, and she seems to step in its place when she takes up all of those wonderful stories. You know, we said to each other, where'd it come from?

Dr. Maya Angelou:

That's exactly right.

---

[1]   The transcription from the tape recording of this conversation indicates that these lines from the poem "Notes on Commercial Theatre," by Langston Hughes, as well as other poems quoted in this conversation, were recited with a few variations from the originals.

Dr. Eleanor Traylor:

Where did that particular kind of genius come from?

Dr. Maya Angelou:

Well, you see, there was a woman born about 1880, which was ten years before it is said that Miss Hurston was born. But then, I wouldn't do too meticulous research on a woman's birth, you know, I just have more grace than that. But she said she was born in 1901, and I take her word for that because my mother used to tell me, any woman who would tell her age would tell anything.

Miss Spencer, Miss Ann Spencer, born around 1880, wrote a poem called "Letter to My Sister," in which she said, it is dangerous for a woman to defy the gods, to taunt them with the tongue's thin tip, or to strut in the weakness of mere humanity, or to draw a line daring them to cross. The gods own the searing lightening, tormenting fears, and the anger of red monthly sins. But much worse if you mince timidly, if you dodge this way or that . . . sweat agony drops, throw your frail body over your feeble young, if you have beauty or none, vowed or celibate, the gods are juggernaut, passing over, passing over. This you may do. Lock your heart, then, quietly, lest they peer within, light no lamp when dark comes down and raise no shade for sun. Breathless must your breath come through if you dare die and deny the gods their god-like fun.

Now, you see, if Miss Ann Spencer wrote that, this is something out of this legacy. Miss Zora Neale Hurston invented herself, you see, I mean, there were women and men, but I am thinking particularly of black women who you were mentioning.

Dr. Eleanor Traylor:

Where's Harriett Jacobs, 1851 or so? Who wrote these lines in that marvelous narrative where she tells the story of her own emancipation of herself? She said: Reader, my story ends with freedom; my children and I are as free as any of the white people of the north. Not to say that that is very much, but she said: The dream of my life has not yet been realized. That's the dream

Dr. Maya Angelou:
This is it—

Dr. Eleanor Traylor:
That Miss Hurston takes up.

Dr. Maya Angelou:
Exactly, exactly, and it is wonderful to me to realize that Zora Neale Hurston wrote of love. Now, it's sad to say, when a number of non-black people write about black people and romantic love, because they are so erroneously informed, they would have us believe that white people make love; black, brown, beige, red, and yellow people just have sex, and that all the time and always successfully. NOT! NOT! So, Miss Hurston wrote about romantic love in the black community, really sweet romance, and it is time for our young men and women to be reminded of the romantic love. Because a people without romance are brutish and rude and crass and shallow, superficial, and really, really, would not last long, will not. We have had romance in the black community so long. During slavery, after that period, that was such a hoax in the nineteenth century. There was a shred of a folk song in which a black man spoke of the woman he loved, and the man said, "The woman I love is fat and chocolate to the bone. And every time she shakes some skinny woman loses her home." [*Laughter.*] That's it, I mean—

Dr. Eleanor Traylor:
I know.

Dr. Maya Angelou:
Miss Hurston, in *Their Eyes Were Watching God*, lets us see romance in the black community, beautiful images of romance, tender and glorious and sensual romance. So as far as I can see, Miss Hurston is the first person who brought the romance in our

community to light. Other than in the music, other than in the lyric, because there was a shred of a folk song in which a black woman spoke of the man she loved and this shred found its way into Mr. W.C. Handy's twentieth century blues. The woman sang, "He's blacker than midnight, teeth like flags of truce, he's the finest thing in the whole St. Louis. They say the blacker the berry, mmm mmm, sweeter is the juice." Now, that is romance.

Well, until Miss Zora Neale Hurston wrote about this, we would have had no occasion to read about it in the literature of the nineteenth century and the early twentieth century, save for in the poetry, in the lyrics of music, the lyrics of songs. Is that right?

Dr. Eleanor Traylor:
Absolutely. Wonderful to bring that thing to fruition as she did. We've had stories of women waking to the reality of themselves and then discovering they're trapped—the horror of their trap—not so, Janie.

Dr. Maya Angelou:
No.

Dr. Eleanor Traylor:
She has it all, and Sister, I like that little twist—there's so much fun in Miss Hurston, there's so much wonder, humor, and fun. In order for Janie to have it all, she just can't have that glorious man alone and that wonderful world that they are wrapped in, the world of story, the world of song, the world of culture, the world of all that, the world of love, she has to have a little money too. And she has it all, that wonderful romance with Tea Cake, she has money in the bank and a house. It's wonderful. So it tastes as sweet as sweet can taste. All of the steps—she doesn't miss a one.

Dr. Maya Angelou:
It's true, she never misses, and this is true. It's amazing for me to come to Orlando, to Eatonville, to this community, and see the people who are honoring Miss Hurston, and I wonder how

much of the material is available. How much do people read of Miss Hurston? It's wonderful to have the T-shirt "Zora" and the banner and the flag, but I wonder, are we reading Miss Hurston really? Really? In truth, the books can make a difference in our lives, and we are desperate. Now, you all know it, and you know it, Sister, we are desperate. The truth is, our communities are dying, our children are running crazy in the streets. We, of all people, are afraid to walk down our streets inhabited by our children.

This is real life, but it's no plaything. We may laugh and joke, but it's no plaything. The children need to read and need to be read to. We desperately need to read Zora Neale Hurston to the children. We need to read Langston Hughes to the children, and County Cullen to the children, and Georgia Douglas Johnson to the children. The children need us, and somehow we have taken our hands out. And yet we come out to celebrate in festival and gala, and sometimes do it superficially, and we have the form and not the fan, the form, the shape. There's a poem of Lucille Clifton which I love, it's called "Miss Rosy." Miss Clifton—who is a current or contemporary Zora Neale Hurston to me—she wrote, "Miss Rosy, when I see you, you black brown red beige yellow white sack of a woman, when I see you wrapped up in your mind like last week's grocery list, I say, Miss Rosy, when I see you in your old man shoes with the big toe cut out, I say, Miss Rosy when I see you who used to be the prettiest gal in Georgia, used to be called Georgia Rose, Miss Rosy, when I see you through your destruction, I stand up."

Now it would seem to me that if we had any sense real sense of survival left, it is through the lives of Fredrick Douglass and Martin King and Malcolm and Zora Neale Hurston, Mary McLeod Bethune—it is through their lives that we begin to see paths, and we have to tell the children these roads. These roads have been laid out for them, and I think it is imperative that we take a Zora Neale and take this kind of weekend and renew ourselves. Isn't it?

Dr. Eleanor Traylor:

It is absolutely true. Three drums played in the work of Miss Hurston. The catacomb drum, for instance, is the drum of praise for the ancestor. There are two others, and I want to talk about that one. That's the drum of praise and triumph for the ancestor, and in the whole scheme of that work there are so many cultural messages. Miss Hurston talks a great deal about children, and in the portraits that she builds in her fictions, in *Jonah's Gourd Vine* and in *Their Eyes Were Watching God,* those marvelous portraits of women, we concentrate on Janie. Janie's beautiful and consummate, but there are other portraits equally glorious. There is the portrait of Amy Pearson, John Pearson's mother in *Jonah's Gourd Vine,* and she tells her husband, "We must love and treasure our children. They are ours for the first time," she said because the man, her husband, Ned, had been born in slavery, she right after that. Our children weren't ours, then they are ours now, and we must love them, we must treasure them. And she talks, Sister, about grown folks who should take for their paradise an example sometimes, the honesty and the courage of children.

Dr. Maya Angelou:

It's been very real. *[Applause.]*

Dr. Eleanor Traylor:

The poetry of Lucy Potts Pearson, when she tells her daughter, you be the bell cow, don't fool around with the tail of things, and all of the wonderful example of that fulfilled life, a life fulfilled in marriage in the home, never mind the sorrows, the sorrows—

Dr. Maya Angelou:

Will come—

Dr. Eleanor Traylor:

You can't have but the joy. It's the anguish and the joy of the blues life. Sister, don't you think that blues, in our terms for contemporary humanity, is the projection of a noble life, just as tragedy was?

Dr. Maya Angelou:
Oh, yes.

Dr. Eleanor Traylor:
Antiquity, I mean as a projection.

Dr. Maya Angelou:
I believe so, and for me poetry has always served the blues and the spirituals. I love to memorize old, old blues, and I hear there's a poem, Paul Laurence Dunbar's poem, which is a refutation that black men don't love their children. And this Mr. Dunbar wrote this poem, it's a blues, for all intents and purposes a pretty blues. He wrote it about 1894, and a black man speaks to his son. He said: Little brown baby with sparkling eyes, come to your papa and sit on his knee. What you been doing, son? Making sand pies. Look at that bib, you as dirty as me, look at those hands, that's molasses I bet. Come here, Miranda, clean off his hands. Boy, the bees are gonna git you and eat you up, being so sticky and sweet, goodness lands. Little brown baby with sparkling eyes, who's papa's darling, who's papa's child? Who never once tries to be cross or lose that smile? Where did you get the teeth? Boy, you a scamp. Where did the dimples come from in your chin? Papa don't know you, I believe you a tramp. Mama, here comes some ole straggler round here, trying to get in. We don't want no stragglers hanging round here, let's give him away to the big bugger man. I know he's hanging around here somewhere. Bugger man, bugger man, come in the door. Here's a little boy to eat. Mama and Papa don't want him no more. Just gobble him up from his head to... I knew that would make you hug me up close. You go away, old bugger, you shan't have this boy. He ain't no straggler, no stranger. Of course, he papa's darling and sweetheart. Enjoy, come to your pallet, darling, go to your rest. I wish you could always know ease and clear skies. I

wish you could just stay a babe on my breast, you little brown baby with sparkling eyes. *[Applause.]*

Dr. Eleanor Traylor:

Sister, Sister, I was almost a pretty big girl before I thought that my grandpa hadn't written that for me.

Dr. Maya Angelou:

But, you see, the children need that, they need portraits which have been written for them. They need desperately, and we have the responsibility of holding those portraits up to the children so that they can know, oh, I've been loved. That's a difference. I've been loved, somebody has cared for me. And you know, we all know that as rough and rude as some of these young men and women are, if we really speak to them the truth . . .

I mean, they say, "Hey, like wait a mo' — I is cool like yo' — "

And you say, "Come here, baby, come here, baby, come here."

"I don't wanna — I mean, like, look here, no."

"Come here, darlin' — come here a minute. Let me speak to you, just let me speak to you."

And before you know it, that same person, all he's been waiting for is somebody to talk to him. "Put your hands on me, touch me, somebody touch me."

So what we got to do is take these positive portraits and show them to the children. Take them to the children in the streets. We've got to do it all. We have to admit all the pain, all the joy, all the triumph, all the overcoming, all the moaning, all the dying, all the standing on slave ships, all the down in the hulls and holes of slave ships, all the standing on slaves, all, all was for nothing, for nothing, for nothing. How can we admit that? How dare we admit that?

Dr. Eleanor Traylor:

We can't admit it, or if we do, we are what Miss Hurston said of someone who almost admitted that, and she was making an example out of that person. He or she was the last stroke of exhausted nature.

Dr. Maya Angelou:
Ooooo.

Dr. Eleanor Traylor:
Ooooo. That's the strongest word in her fiction.

Dr. Maya Angelou:
That's some strong word, exhausted nature?

Dr. Eleanor Traylor:
Of exhausted nature.

Dr. Maya Angelou:
I wouldn't want to admit that to my own self in the privacy of my own private mind, no.

Dr. Eleanor Traylor:
She was doing a little signifying there.

Dr. Maya Angelou:
But she was a great signifier

Dr. Eleanor Traylor:
Oh, she was a great signifier, or whatever.
Dr. Maya Angelou:
And the old people say signifying is worse than stealing.

Dr. Eleanor Traylor:
Exactly [laughter], she was.

Dr. Maya Angelou:
Miss Hurston could signify. I do love the fact, though, that to see you, who I accept as you may not actually be a genius, I mean you might not, but it's close enough for rock and roll. [Laughter.] So to know that you employ that powerful brain and all that training onto the subject of Miss Zora Neale Hurston's magic and mastery is heartening to me, and I know it's heartening to all of us

who love Miss Hurston. I want to say thank you, Sister, thank you.

Dr. Eleanor Traylor:
Thank you, thank you, thank you.

Dr. Maya Angelou:
Now, let's talk some more. Tell me something.

Dr. Eleanor Traylor:
I was just marveling because, as I said, her seventh dream is realized in us, and it's true, because the revelation of the seventh dream was the promise of a complete resurrection, a complete re-creation of immortality. I just looked cursorily at statistics from 1990 to the present time. Sixty thousand copies of *Their Eyes*, thirty thousand of *Jonah's Gourd*, thirty-one thousand of *Tell My Horses* — just incredible, the availability of all that lifesaving, wondrous work, all that work which raises, as you say, the issues before us now.

Dr. Maya Angelou:
That's right.

Dr. Eleanor Traylor:
The issues before us now.

Dr. Maya Angelou:
It is wonderful to commend and celebrate that spirit and that intelligence and that courage and that art. It is wonderful to celebrate it now, but if it is not applicable in our lives today, then it is of no use — it's a metaphor, it's all for show, and nice and thank you very much and good night, Nurse, you know. But if we really see it as usable . . . Robert Hayden, speaking of Fredrick Douglass, said, "When it is finally ours, this beautiful and terrible thing more needful to man than air, more usable than earth, when it is more than the gaudy mumbo-jumbo of politicians, when it is more than diastole and systole, when it belongs at last to our children, then you know it's a work. And this is true for Miss

Hurston. When we can really use the portraits and employ them to help our children stand erect and know something about themselves, then her life has not been in vain, nor her death.

Dr. Eleanor Traylor:
Absolutely not, and then not her death, but in the discovery that there can be no death.

Dr. Maya Angelou:
Be no death, yes this is true.

Dr. Eleanor Traylor:
With production like that, when you hand it over, when you put those stories into the hands of the young, where you put them into the hands of the old—Sister, I want to tell an anecdote.

Dr. Maya Angelou:
Please. I bet you will. *[Laughter.]*

Dr. Eleanor Traylor:
I went to Haiti with Dr. Long and the conference of African American Culture. There in Haiti we were invited by the then-curator of the museum, Dr. Pierre Man Hacia, to dinner. When I arrived in his house, I was as stunned as I was when I arrived in the museum. What he had was a collection of the carnival art of Haiti, paper maché of pieces, icons, beautiful, and I admired them so. Dr. Man Hacia said, "You may have one," and he said, "Just select," and I did. I selected one, then I changed my mind and I selected another, and he said, "Have what you will." I brought it home and that year was not too good of a year, Sister. Things happened. Amenia Dickerson is in this room she can bear me out.

One night, a particularly anguished night, I was reading *Tell My Horse*, a gift from a student of mine. The book had been reissued. And as I read through, I discovered what I had brought home. I had brought home Danbala, the god of creativity, but there are two, Miss Hurston said. One is destructive, and the other is the essence of construction. I had selected first the construction, then the destruction; I had brought destruction in my house. And Miss Hurston said that night "Now get it out," and I did. I called Amenia Dickerson and said, "Does the Museum of African Art want it?" and Amenia said, "Leave it where it is." And that is what we did. So I mean the absolutely ongoing instruction of the woman in everything, in every facet, and for everyone.

Dr. Maya Angelou:

Now, brothers and sisters, there is something going on, and I think we will best serve ourselves. If there is a doctor in the house, will he or she come forward, please. Here's one, here's two. Thank you. Thank you. Now, brothers and sisters, ladies and gentlemen, we will serve ourselves best if we contain ourselves in our thoughts. And we will serve this person who is in distress best if we contain ourselves best in our thoughts. We may send our thoughts of strength and saving to the person, but let us use our energies now--please, not as looky-loos hello! [Applause and laughter.]

All right. It is possible, as you know, Sister, and your story showed very clearly, it is possible to have a negative in your life. A part of our history tells us what happens when we keep the negative. The negative Danbala, or the negative in our lives, what has happened to us historically, has been the employment of an idea which was really Machiavellian, which was he wrote in about 1500, in which he told the power of the time how to control the people, and he said, if you will control them, separate them and rule them, divide them and you can conquer them. This has been successfully employed against us, and we have used it, we have kept that negative in our spirit, in our home, in our community, and in our mouths, and you know it. Separate and rule, divide and conquer.

If we are to survive at all, we have to do what Dr. Traylor did and take that negative Danbala out of the house, out of minds, out of mouths, because what happens is, the children see it, and so the children—we say, my Dr. Haodoweaiht is—oh, yes, my preacher, my So-and-So. Oh, look at him, he's dark but he is nice looking.

Listen to it. The truth is a stubborn fact. Look at it. So then the kid gets up in the morning and looks in the mirror as he brushes his teeth, and says, "Jesus, I'm the very spitting image of the very thing my parents hate, the very thing they despise." And then we say, "Go out and run the ten-yard dash and bring me back the gold cup, go out and go to school and bring me back A's." How can they? We have included between our teeth, like grits of sand, the very negative thing that will kill us. We have got to oust it. You put it out of your house? We've got to put it out of our houses. We've got to, or we will be dead. You see the children—I know, I don't want to beat a dead horse. The truth is, we have not come here just to extol Zora Neale Hurston or any writer or any preacher or teacher or any rabbi or any priest. It's not just for that. If it is of any use at all, it is to encourage the race to continue. To continue with some passion, if it is of any use. It is to encourage us to continue with passion, some compassion, some humor, and some style. That's it, or what's it all about, Elsie. It's a joke.

Dr. Eleanor Traylor:
    Absolutely

Dr. Maya Angelou:
    It is an intellectual exercise otherwise. Thank you very much. Am I to read this? Thank you.

    There is a medical emergency, and we will ask you to please sit for a few minutes while this is taken care of. We will have a short break of about maybe 15 minutes while they take the person in distress out. I do believe that prayers are things . . . I do believe that. I have seen it. I have lived this long and seen the effect of prayers. I would ask, although very few of us would know this person who is in physical distress, I would ask you just to spend a second, to think him or her very good thoughts. It liberates. Just continue? You know it wouldn't be a bad idea if we turn the lights on out there and ask people for a couple of questions.

Dr. Eleanor Traylor:

It would be wonderful, but could I ask you just one thing? I just wanted to comment when you said looky-loos, you were so much like Miss Hurston, continuing that tradition of a wonderful kind of critique as you were making and wonderful new language, just inventing new language like Mouth Almighty. You know, Miss Hurston would say, "Look at Mouth Almighty sitting on the porch, just criticizing everything, can always tear down but never build." It's wonderful.

Dr. Maya Angelou:

Because I know you all are here with the mind to celebrate, I think it is also a good idea to exchange ideas, so if you have one question maybe we can ask you for it, and Dr. Traylor and I will mull over it. *[Laughter.]* If you don't, it's okay. I have lots I wanna tell you about.

Now, it would seem, looking at the panoply of women writers, Miss Hurston stepped on the shoulders of a lot of ladies, a lot of wonderful writing women, including Georgia Douglas Johnson, who I wanted to speak about. Miss Johnson, she's my favorite, but then I'm fickle. She's my favorite right-now poet, but in about fifteen minutes I'll say somebody else I know. I'm not very stable.

But, Miss, she wrote this beautiful love poem. I want to die while you love me, while yet you hold me fair, while laughter lies upon my lips and lights are in my hair. I want to die while you love me. Who would care to live till love has nothing more to ask and nothing more to give? I want to die while you love me and bear to that still bed, your kisses turbulent, unspent to warm me when I'm dead. Mmm mmmm mmm.

Now, Miss Hurston, as the poet said, had some sturdy black britches to stand up on and then a number of us writers following have stood upon her shoulders. So I mean, Miss Alice Walker says so. And I know Bell Hooks has been here. She's here? Oh, Lord. Are you really? Well, bless your heart. I know Beverly Sheftall, Guy Sheftall was here. She's here? That's it, a number of us, and certainly Rosa Guy and all black ladies. Barbara Christian? These are some deep, deep. . . . Our way is clear. Miss Hurston's shoulders are very broad and very strong and insouciant. Isn't that a nice word?

Sassy, that reminds me of Mari Evans. Mari Evans wrote, Where have you gone, why did you leave me, where have you gone with your confident walk and crooked smile? Are you aware that when you left, with you went the sun, the moon, and what few stars there are, where you have gone with your confident walk and your crooked smile, with you went my heart in one pocket and the rent money in the other. *[Laughter and applause.]*

A while ago, Dr. Traylor mentioned the humor with which Miss Hurston employed all the time, sometimes a bitter humor, but always humor, and I never trust people who don't laugh, personally. People who act as if they put airplane glue on the back of their hand and stuck them to their forehead—they didn't come to stay, they didn't come to make a difference. So, Miss Hurston, sometimes it shocks you, when you are reading her, to find her humor in a very tragic situation, but that's when you need it, isn't it?

Dr. Eleanor Traylor:
Oh, yeah.

Dr. Maya Angelou:
I know that a number of people who are not blessed with my particular racial heritage find it very strange when black people laugh. They say, "God, what are you laughing about?" And people say, "Ooooo, this is so, too, I can't stand it, it's so bad, it's so bad, I mean it just cracks me up, it's so bad." So a number of people with other heritages look and say, "What can you find to laugh about?" Zora Neale Hurston said, "Now, here is the lie." She was talking about telling stories. She said, "Here is the lie that is beyond suspicion, I mean this is some deep lie now here. But if you don't laugh you will die anyway."

Well, I like that, and I also love her love of love. I know there is an African statement, "I don't trust people who don't love themselves." It's dangerous, because the person may say he or she loves me or loves you. What they really mean is that they want to possess, to have some of that. There's an African saying which is "Be careful when a naked person offers you a shirt." It's true, because if he had something he would put it on himself first.

I love that in her, and also — maybe this should be primary — the courage, the courage to see and say what you saw. It is said that courage is the most important of all the virtues because without courage you can't practice any other virtue consistently, you can't be consistently fair or kind or generous or just or merciful, not without courage. Not consistently. Oh, you can do it sporadically, time in and time out, but to do it continually, you have to have courage. And maybe this is the most important of Miss Hurston's gifts, the application of courage to see and say what you saw, even when she was wrong, stand up akimbo and say it. I mean that liberates. It has to liberate, it's meant to liberate. Yes. . . . Did somebody have a question?

Dr. Eleanor Traylor:

I thought someone did, from the back.

Dr. Maya Angelou:

Yes please? Okay, all right, thank you. I heard it. I'm young. *[Laughter.]*

The speaker said she is a future educator and is interested in educating in multi-cultural information and would like to know — what do we have to say to young would-be teachers to encourage them and prepare them to overcome the negative stereotypes? Is that right? Hello! I don't have an answer but I heard it! *[Laughter.]*

No, wait, wait. Well, my dear daughter, I would encourage you and all teachers to be Black teachers, White, Asian, Spanish-speaking, Native American, Alley Oop, all to read, read without ceasing, read everything, everything you can, read the Russian writers, read the African writers, read the African American writers, read the Asian writers. Be conversant, know as much as possible. All knowledge is dispensable, depending on the market. Put it in the brain. Put it in, load it. Everything you put in will only cover one corner. If you work your lifetime, you can't possibly know enough, so read and try to retain so that you have something to say to the children. And not just the mumbo-jumbo, not just what seems comfortable and easy. Read it all, know so much. Try to be like Richard Long, wherever he is in this place. Richard Long is the only polymath I know, which means he knows a lot about everything, and will tell you whether you are right or not. *[Laughter.]* That's my first encouragement, to know so much that you are at ease and you don't have to hate anybody just cuz you don't know what they know. Do you understand? Okay. *[Applause.]* Sister, would you add to that?

Dr. Eleanor Traylor:
Oh, Sister, I would just add to that only one thing, that you have so many resources at your disposal within your culture. Miss Hurston sat on the gateposts of Eatonville and saw the world right inside the experience of this people. We are told that if you want to educate human beings, you must have the vision to understand that the whole process must lead to what Mr. Dubois called broad sympathy. Just an embrace of the world. Broad sympathy, knowledge of the world that was and is and our relation to that world. Everyone has his own, her own relation to the world. Every culture has its own relation to the world. What is it that you yourself can give your children? What is it that you can inspire in them to give to the world? You know, if we just stay on that subject, we will have it licked. The underlying thing that we all have to give is something that this literature, this culture talks a lot about, and that's love. That was Miss Hurston's subject.

Dr. Maya Angelou:
Well, well. That's fantastic, it's true. And let me add to that, that does not mean indulgence, it does not mean sentimentality. It doesn't mean mush. Love is that condition in the human spirit so

profound that it encourages us to develop courage and to use that courage to build bridges and to cross those bridges in an attempt to reach other human beings. That's what love is. It's probably that condition which causes the stars to remain in the firmament, and molecules to move around each other with some kind of appearance of grace. Probably it is phenomenal. It is not indulgence.

Dr. Eleanor Traylor:
And cannot be moved, Sister?

Dr. Maya Angelou:
And shall not be moved, yes. Well, my grandmother raised me in a little village in Arkansas, about the size of this part of the stage. And Momma used to sing, Momma, you oughta see Momma, you oughta all know Momma. Momma, we all have her, him, papa, uncle, because each one of us has been paid for. It's very important to remember that, whether the ancestors came from Ireland in the 1840s or 1950s, trying to escape the potato blight, or if they came from Eastern Europe, trying to escape the Pogroms, arriving at Ellis Island, having their names changed to something utterly unpronounceable, or if they came from Asia in the 1850s to build this country, to build the railroad, unable legally to bring their mates for eight or nine decades, or if they came from South America, trying to find a place that would hold all the people, or if they came from Africa, lying spoon-fashion in the filthy hatches of slave ships, and in their own and each other's excrement and urine—they have paid for each of us already. It's important to know that. So that we can look at the mommas and the papas and the uncles and the aunties and the grandmas and grandpas with some appreciation, some tenderness, some love, and we can say with my grandmother who used to sing, "I shall not be moved." When she died she was over six foot, and she whispered all the time. I remember people looking at the table and look over to Momma, big lady, and say what you say, Sister. .
. .

But in church on Sunday, Lord! I stayed with her for ten years, and every Sunday, after about fifteen minutes, the preacher would say, "We will be led in a song from Sister Henderson," and my grandmother would say, "Me?" And when you are young, nobody can embarrass you so much as an adult to whom you are related, right in public? I would just sit there, dying. I would think, Momma, get up and sing. Everybody knows you gonna sing. They even know what you're gonna sing. Momma, get up and sing. The children in the children's pew would be just sliding off the bench, saying, "Your grandma's doing it again." I was mortified, but finally she'd get up and sing. And when she sang, this huge voice would come out, and momma could sing so at least once or twice, every two or three months, some woman in the church would get happy and wind up her purse and just throw it at the preacher, *whap!*

Momma used to sing this song. She sang, "I shall not, I shall not be removed." I couldn't talk—it was during a period when I didn't talk—so I would write, "It is not removed, Momma." Momma would put her glasses on. She'd say, "Yeah, Sister, Momma know, I shall not, I shall not be removed."

This poem came directly out of seminar at which Dr. Eleanor Traylor spoke in my town in North Carolina many years ago. It was her look at the African American women and all women who tried so hard to hold their loves and beloved together. It is also an honor to Toni Cade Bambara, because of something you said that particular day.

She lay, skin down in the moist dirt, the canebreak rustling with the whispers of leaves, and the loud longing of hounds and the ransack of hunters crackling the near branches.

She muttered, lifting her head a nod toward freedom, I shall not, I shall not be moved.

She gathered her babies, their tears slick as oil on black faces, their young eyes canvassing mornings of madness. Momma, is Master gonna sell you from us tomorrow?

Yes. Unless you keep walking more and talking less. Yes. Unless the keeper of our lives releases me from all commandments. Yes. And your lives, never mine to live, will be executed upon the killing floor of innocents. Unless you match my heart and words and say with me,

I shall not, I shall not be moved.

In Virginia tobacco fields, along Arkansas roads, in the red hills of Georgia, into the palms of her chained hands, she cried against calamity, you have tried to destroy me and though I perish daily,

I shall not I shall not be moved.

Her universe, summarized into one black body falling finally from the tree to her feet, made her cry each time in a new voice. All my paths hasten to defeat, strangers claim the glory of my love, inequity has bound me to his bed.

yet, I shall not, I shall not be moved.

She heard the names, swirling ribbons in the wind of history: nigger, nigger bitch, heifer, mammy, property, creature, ape, baboon, whore, hot tail, thing, it. She said, But my description cannot fit your tongue, for I have a certain way of being in this world,

I shall not I shall not be moved.

No angel stretched protecting wings above the heads of her children, fluttering and urging the winds of reason into the confusions of their lives. They sprouted like young weeds, but she could not shield their growth from the grinding blades ignorance, nor shape them into symbolic topiaries. She sent them away, underground, overland, in coaches, barefoot.

She said, When you get, give. When you learn, teach. As for me,

I shall not, I shall not be moved.

She stood in mid-ocean, seeking God's face. Assured, she placed her fire of service on the altar, and although closed in the finery of Semite and faith, when she appeared at the temple door, no sign welcomed Black Grandmother, Come in here.

Into that raging crashing ignorance, she cried, No one, no, nor no one million ones dare to deny me God. I enter into the tents of forgiveness.

The divine upon my right impels me to pull forever on the latch of Freedom's gate.

The Holy Spirit upon my left sends my feet without ceasing into the camp of the righteous the tents of the free.

These momma faces, these grandmamma faces, lemon yellow, plum-purple, honey-brown, have grimaced and twisted down a pyramid of years. She is Sheba the Sojourner, Harriet and Zora.

Today she stands before the abortion clinic, confounded by her lack of choices. In the Welfare line, reduced to the pity of handouts, ordained in the pulpit, shielded by mystery. In operating rooms, husbanding life. In the choir loft, holding God in her throat. On street corners hawking her body. In the classroom, loving children to understanding.

Centered on the world's stage, she sings to her loves and beloveds, to her foes and detractors: However I am conceived, or deceived, or perceived, however my ignorance and conceit, lay aside your fears that I will be undone,

I shall not, I shall not be moved. I shall not, I shall not be moved. Just like a tree that's planted by the water, oh, I shall not be moved.

[Applause.]

Thank you. Thank you.

Patricia Merritt Watson:

If any one wonders what to teach the children, teach them that poem. Thank you all for coming you have been a great audience, but you had great people. *[Applause.]*

Am I proud to be a sister this evening? Yes I am, among these two very strong living legends, dynamic women full of love, romance, and life. Will I have a message for my children in the morning? Yes I will. Will you? You may be seated. We thank Mrs. N. Y. Nathiri and Mrs. Dexter from the bottom of our hearts. We thank the entire Festival of the Arts and Humanities, our special guests this evening, the participants who have given of their time and research, the Eatonville community, educational and private sponsors. We thank all of you, the Hurston family who support us and those who have traveled from great places and not so great places. Good evening.

[Applause.]

Dr. Maya Angelou

]

Dr. Maya Angelou (center)

Hurston family members

Jazz singer Jacqueline Jones

Actor Richard Roundtree with University of Central Florida students

Mosella Wells leading an Ecumenical Worship Service.

Great Ribs!

Education Day activities

Zora Neale Hurston from
a Global Perspective:
Yuji Maekawa and Asha S. Kanwar
Moderated by Ronald Foreman

Professor Yuji Maekawa from Hiroshima Jogakwin College, Japan, and Professor Asha S. Kanwar from Indira Gandhi National Open University, India, participated in the fifth annual Zora Neale Hurston Festival of the Arts and Humanities in 1994. The discussion was moderated by Dr. Ronald Foreman from the University of Florida, Gainesville.

Dr. Foreman:

We appreciate the extension of the presence of those of you who were here before and welcome others who were not here for the first session. This is, I think, very, very important, because the idea is to look at how some of our colleagues from places throughout and around the world may have a particular view of Zora Hurston's works, her life, her writings.

This is marvelous, that there is an extension that is intercontinental, because it suggests there will be opportunities for some of us to use some library resources and see some colleagues in places that we had not thought about. At the same time, we want to welcome our colleagues from abroad. We have Dr. Yuji Maekawa, who is going to give a presentation. He is from Japan, but at the moment is visiting scholar at the University of Florida in Gainesville, and we are very happy to have him down here in Eatonville on this occasion. And we also have Professor

Asha Kumar, and she is going to share with you information that she has vis-à-vis a title she will give you at the time she does the presentation, which will be in order. I'm going to ask both of our colleagues to allow some time or gain for the kind of interesting commentary that we had in the previous session. Thank you.

Dr. Yuji Maekawa:

Thank you very much, Dr. Foreman, and good morning, everyone. Thank you for coming, since this is the first time for me to read my paper in overseas country, so I am very nervous and now can understand a professional boxer's feelings. It is often said that it is difficult to get the championship belt overseas country. *[Laughter.]* I don't plan on getting the championship belt, but like a boxer I feel very nervous now. In addition to that, I am a foreigner, so I am afraid my English will not be understood by you, but I try to read my paper as clearly as possible and slowly as possible, so please try to understand my English. After our session our paper will have some period to discuss, so please give us some comments or advice and it will be very helpful for future research.

Today I'd like to give a presentation from the viewpoint of a foreigner, in particular as one of a Japanese reader. The title of my presentation is "Zora and Yanagita." Yanagita is the ethnologist's name, so just to keep in your mind I often use his name Yanagita. The subtitle is "Theory of Coexistence." My main purpose is to put an emphasis on similarity between Zora and Yanagita and to show that Zora's world is applicable not only to America or African America or Africa, but also to other worlds, especially Japan's world. Yesterday, the focus of the presentation was on African continuity or African heritage. I am interested in that topic and what I am going to explain today is about that topic. Since I am going to explain it from a different point of view, I will not use those terms, but the content of my presentation is around that topic. So this is important for you to understand about my presentation.

First of all, let me explain my personal interest in black literature. Very briefly, it started [when I was] a college student. There was a professor specialist in black literature who affected me very much. First I was interested in William Faulkner and wrote a thesis with the title "Faulkner and Black People" in Japanese. As a graduate student I focused on James Baldwin. My interest in Zora Neale Hurston began much later. In 1984 I happened to [see] the name Alice Walker in the newspaper which introduced her popular movie *The Color Purple* in the United States. I felt very interested in Alice Walker, and in 1986 I wrote my first paper on Alice Walker. While I was working on Alice Walker, I found Zora's name in her essays. In 1990 I wrote my first paper on Hurston with a title of "A Study of Zora Neale Hurston and Zora and Her Works." This is a kind of introductory paper. I have been working on her since then.

When I first read *Their Eyes Were Watching God*, I was very impressed. My way of reading this novel was from the viewpoint that Janie's trying to keep herself as an individual like a modern hero or heroine. In addition, I gradually came to understand that she's recognizing black people's identity in African continuity, but at the same time my impression was that her final goal would not be African identity or African continuity. The reason for that impression is that there is something familiar to the Japanese people, somewhere in her works.

First of all, I'd like to show you some of these examples of familiarity to Japanese people. In *Jonah's Gourd Vine*, when Lucy is dying, what people in her neighborhood do for her is very similar to those customs in Japan. There used to be many midwives like Aunt Finnie in Japan. Even if they were not qualified midwives, women in the neighborhood had enough knowledge of midwives, and also grandmothers acted as midwives.

In Chapter Four of *Tell My Horse*, the custom that liquor is given to [the dead] in the tomb is explained. In Japan we have the same custom, giving Saki—this is Japanese liquor or wine made from rice—so, giving Saki to the tombstone. Sometimes water is given. Also to give some food in order to make him happy is very similar to customs in Japan. They regard the dead answers to us as gods, and there exist other gods such as the Sun God, the Water God, and Nature God. We can read these scenes with full understanding.

The contents of tall tales and whole structure with call and response in the first part of *Mules and Men* are also familiar. We still keep this kind of custom, too, in our daily life. In addition I have the impression that Zora's word is similar to Kunio Yanagita—Kunio is his first name and Yanagita is his family name—Kunio Yanagita's word. He is a Japanese ethnologist. Next I'll give you a very brief introduction about him, but today I would like to make an analogy between Zora and Yanagita, and to explain what Zora said.

Okay, let me explain very briefly about Yanagita. It is commonly recognized that he is the first and the greatest ethnologist in Japan. He was born in Hyogo Prefecture, West Japan, in 1875. As a student at Tokyo Imperial University, which is the former University of Tokyo, he studied agriculture administration and learned to see things from the ordinary people's point of view. In 1910, when he was 35 years old, he published *The Legends of Tono*. This is also very important term for my presentation, Legends of Tono. I will explain a little bit about this later. When I compare him with Zora, I like to use this book as an object of comparison.

What is *The Legends of Tono*? Very brief introduction about this book. It was published in 1910. Yanagita wrote down what one of his friends who lived in Tono—Tono is the name of place— told him: each legend has a number from one through 119; however, in contents, forty-one titles are listed as titles like index. Under each title, the number of each legend is written. Some legends are independent, but others are interdependent. The structure of each legend is not dialogue, but monologue.

Okay, let's go to the comparison between Zora and Yanagita. Both Yanagita and Zora paid attention to the importance of folk culture, even while not many took it worthy of notice. In the preface of the original edition of *The Legends of Tono*, he says, "I think a book like *Legends of Tono* goes against present-day literary fashions." In 1935 he republished it and said in memorandum for that edition, "Actually, when *The Legends of Tono* was first published, society did not know that this kind of thing had even existed, and it seemed they criticized the attitude of one person who tried to think much of this as a weird and selfish thing. However, today the trend of the time is completely different." We can learn from these quotations that there was a tendency that most people in Japan's society did not recognize folk culture as real culture, and why he wrote *The Legends of Tono*. In case of Zora, in the 1920s more anthropologists around her came to pay attention to native culture. However, they still had an ethnocentric bias because the attitude to native culture was to judge it as primitive, since it was not white nor European. In addition, it was in the 1930s and 1940s—the best days for the protest novelist, when she published *Their Eyes Were Watching God*—she says in *Dust Tracks on a Road*, "From what I had read and heard, Negros were supposed to write about the race problem," because to write about traditional black people, folk culture was considered to degrade the black people, even though it was the day when native and ordinary people's culture was not given proper evaluation. Both Yanagita and Zora thought each culture had its own value itself, and that it should not be evaluated in contrast with another culture.

We can find some stories which are common between Yanagita and Zora. One of the most interesting common factors is the way of dealing with nature and the author's attitude toward God. In both cases the relations between human beings and animals are often described so as to show that people are in harmony with the reason of nature. Zora writes in *Mules and Men* that the mockingbirds help the murderer who descended into hell. She also writes the man who ignored the preacher's advice and went fishing on the Sabbath day, was pulled down into the river by a catfish, and died. In addition, she writes that people take advantage of nature, like the man who cut the possum's tail from which he made strings for banjo. We can also find the stories which show close relations between human life and animals by personification of animals. The examples for this, "How Br'er Dog Lost His Beautiful Voice" in chapter 7 of *Mules and Men,* and "Why the Dog Hates the Cat" in chapter 10 of *Mules and Men.* Even though we praise the animals in those stories, with human beings we can say that they are not different from the original ones. She tries to give people a lesson about human life.

In Yanagita's stories many animals are described too. For example, a Japanese unique enigmatic water creature, Kappa, is described. It plays a trick on people, so after chastising or reasoning with it, people set it free. Sometimes it makes a young girl pregnant. We can read the stories about the wolf as well; it is depicted as a symbol of wonder. The wolf causes precaution for immoral people because of punishing the immoral. The stories about the relations between people and monkeys, foxes, bears, and birds are described as well. These stories tell us that human life was made in harmony with nature. Even though nature sometimes makes human beings undergo hardships, it is not the object for them to control. They try to accept nature as it really is and to leave their body and everything about themselves to nature. In their world there is no competitive theory, like which is the winner or the loser, but only the theory of coexistence.

People should be harmonious with nature, according to Zora and Yanagita, who fear and respect nature. In [their writing] nature shows its power to the full. In Zora and Yanagita, a snake is sometimes used as an ominous omen and a frog is taken as a rain omen. In Yanagita's world, a fox usually plays the role of snaring human beings. From these examples we can say that they deal with things in nature, not just of things, but of things with souls.

In Japan, especially mountains play very important roles. Ronald A. Morse, who is a translator of *The Legend of Tono* from Japanese to English, explained that mountains have very important meanings in religion in Japan. We can understand his opinion when we see the shrines in mountains and also simple god shelves where people believe gods live. In the case of Yanagita, mountains play very important roles. For example the 32 story in *The Legends of Tono* [tells] that the white deer died and became a mountain god. Furthermore in the 107 and 108 stories, a mountain god gives special power to people. Let me show the example from 107. "In Kamigo village, there is a house that is called the house by the river, which is on the bank of the Hiasee River. One day a young daughter from this house went to the edge of the river and picked up some pebbles. A man she had never seen before gave her some tree leaves and things. He was tall and had a red complexion. The daughter from this day on had the power of divination." This *gaijin*, which means stranger, this *guijin* was a mountain *kami*. *Kami* means "god mountain." It is said that she thus became a child of the mountain *kami*, mountain god. Zora [writes], in *Moses Man of the Mountain*, that Moses is given a special power from the mountain god. Zora's idea is closely related to Yanagita's idea.

In the world we can say that the idea that spirits exist in nature is developed into the one that the things in nature play a role of god and affect people. In *Tell My Horse* we can find many gods which are related to this idea. Rod and Petrol are the typical examples, and Laco Atiso serving Legubar is the god of medicine and knowledge. Shangrol is the god of thunder. Papa Gred is a storm with a spirit. These examples can be considered as the ones to explain nature worship. Even in Japan society there used to be a strong belief that souls dwell in nature long ago. For instance on New Year's Day we used to lay *omochi*, which means rice cake, not only at family Buddhist altar, but in the kitchen and even at the toilet—can you believe it? Some families still do this and further more when we went to the mountains we often found statue of the deity and small and compact *kamidana* shelf of god on our way. In the mountains we could easily find a kind of god house where mountain gods were understood to come and rest.

It is getting difficult now to find these scenes in Japan, even though we have the concept of multi-gods subconsciously. It looks still possible to find these in Southeast Asian countries. They worship the things with spirits in nature, which is called P, which is a godlike existence. It is difficult for those who have

European Christian values to understand the way of thinking, that there exist things with spirits here and there in daily life. It is natural that the world of polytheism is hardly understood in a society where people believe in monotheism. They basically have different criteria for each other. It is not too much to say that the way of human life would be greatly different depending on whether they acknowledge the existence of several gods.

The world of monotheism is basically the place where the existence of other [deities] can be scarcely accepted. The reason will be clearer when we remember that the Christian minister cannot say you can worship Jesus Christ, Buddha, or Mohammed or anyone you like as an object of worship. In the case of polytheism, there is enough room in mind to admit the existence of other [deities], that is to say, in the world of polytheism the theory of co-existence can be more consolidated. We can find the theory of co-existence in Zora's and Yanagita's attitudes as writers. Each story in *The Legends of Tono* was told by Sasaki, but it is re-described with Yanagita's own sense. However, Yanagita seems [intent] to transmit each story, which was told and retold for generations, as precisely as it was transmitted. He writes in the preface of the original edition of *The Legend of Tono*, "All of the tales and stories recorded here were told to me by Mr. Kizen Sasaki, who comes from Tono. I have been writing the stories down as they were told to me during his many evening visits since February 1909."

We can say that Yanagita's attitude, in offering raw materials as they are to readers, is very similar to Zora's attitudes, in *Mules and Men* and *Tell My Horse* in particular. Zora tries to tell what she saw and heard as it was. Her attitude is explained in Rampersad's forward for *Mules and Men*: "Above all, some readers find Hurston insufficiently analytical. . . . Her approach, some would say, was journalistic rather than scientific. . . ." Amelia Mary Adams says almost the same thing about Zora, as follows: "Hurston sat back and told a story in the words of the people. By omitting the layer of outside interpretation, Hurston allowed the reader to be on the culture directly from the speaker. This idea, that the people can define their community and culture values, is one of the principles of native anthropology." This is Zora's coherent attitude as a writer.

By taking an attitude of writing as it is, Zora and Yanagita can have more possibility to co-exist with something different. Both Yanagita's and Zora's intention is to make readers complete their own picture by giving them pieces of stories. We will be convinced when we see that each story is not given any titles on purpose. The titles are shown in the contents, but they are not put at the beginning of each story. For example, Yanagita intends to make readers who read the stories about the village of Tono construct their own village called Tono. In the case of Zora, she wants to lead her readers to rebuild their own African American society with Africanity by showing them African stories one by one.

That is to say, by depicting as it is, the authors can give life to those who transmit stories because their stories are described by the authors. The authors can give vividness to themselves because they are retelling stories to their readers. In addition, the readers can give life to themselves because they are reconstructing their own world with those stories. Since their works are depicted as they really are, people related to the works can keep their own world. We can say that the theory of co-existence is playing a very important role here because each [reader] can construct his or her own world through Zora's and Yanagita's works.

When we read the stories in which Yanagita and Zora explain the relations between nature and human beings, what is more interesting is that both of them have an idea that the dead, the dead people, become a part of nature.

For instance, in Yanagita's fifty-first story, an otobird—*oto* means an onomatopoeia-like word of husband in Japanese—an otobird is depicted. Once upon a time, the daughter of a *choja*—which means a rich man—a daughter of *choja* went off wandering in the mountains one day with her boyfriend. She got lost and became an otobird while she was looking for him. Now she is singing "*atong, atong.*"

Zora writes a story about a bird in "How the Squinch Owl Came to Be" in Chapter Ten of *Mules and Men.* Miss Pheenie, old spinster, was cheated and frozen to death. She took the shape of an owl after she died.

They think that the world after death exists in nature, where the souls of the dead continue to stay. In addition, what is more interesting is that Zora and Yanagita [write] that people in this world can have communication with the dead.

In Zora's work, man exists in this world even after death. In *Tell My Horse* there is such a story told, that salt should not be used at a funeral. In *Jonah's Gourd Vine,* people believed that the head of the dead should be directed toward the east and the pillow should be taken away from the dead too. In "Spunk," Zora describes the scene [where] Joe, who was killed, was reborn as a bobcat and revenged himself on Spunk. These examples tell us that her world is constructed with her strong consciousness that there exists a world after death. Actually, she says in *Tell My Horse,* "It all stems from the firm belief in survival after death, or rather that there is no death."

Yanagita also writes a story [in which] a man meets a dead person [who] continues to live as a spirit of the mountain, or to live as a god of the mountain, watching village people. Again, in *The Legends of Tono,* Cuji, a son of a scholar, got married but lost his wife [when] a tsunami took her away. One year later, he met his wife on the beach.

To both [Yanagita and Zora], the dead are not non-existing but existing. The dead continue to exist in this world with the same or different appearances, having communication with the people. What Zora and Yanagita are doing as writers, in other words, writing works on the basis of historical oral tradition, is having communication with the dead.

One of the characteristics of *The Legends of Tono* is that Yanagita introduces stories told by Kizen Kasaki, one of

Yanagita's friends living in Tono. In addition, Otto, who wrote comment at the end of recent edition of *The Legends of Tono,* says, "Stories in *The Legends of Tono* were the ones that Mr. Sasaki heard himself and the ones which were told traditionally in that place. Some of them are the stories about the relatives of the Sasakis, his friends, and the experiences of Sasaki himself." He wants to say that there were some people who had told the stories to Mr. Sasaki before he told them to Yanagita. We can say that the oral tradition plays a very important role in Yanagita's world. The stories in *The Legends of Tono* are the ones which have been transmitted from people to people for several generations.

The same thing can be said for Zora, too. In *Mules and Men* and *Tell My Horse,* she introduces the stories which were told by people around her. Also, the whole structure of *Their Eyes were Watching God* is supported by the pattern [in which] Janie tells the stories to Phoebe and Phoebe tells Janie's stories to Zora and Zora tells those stories to her readers and readers tell stories to next person and next person and so on.

That is to say, in both Yanagita's and Zora's cases, oral tradition plays an important role which is the fundamental structure of their works. When we trace back stories that have been told and retold for generations, we will be able to reach our ancestors. So to tell and retell folk tales is to have communication with ancestors, and to call back ancestors to the present world as well. What we have to pay attention [to] now is that both Zora and Yanagita do not regard the dead people as past beings. They believe that the dead people are still alive in the present world. They can have this belief because they have a different concept of time.

We chronologically divide and classify time into the past, present, and future. On the other hand, they do not take time as separate, but consider it as unified. The chronological time concept tends to cause people to make things classified. For instance, in our daily example, people are apt to give priority to new things and to the earlier arrival as a contest. If time is taken not as a chronological set but as a unity, we can say that it becomes impossible to make the usual distinction of time. Then what has been denied, on the basis of priority of time concept, will recover the right to exist. Those who have been regarded as losers, according to the criteria of chronological time concept, will be able to tear off their titles of losers. We can understand that without chronological time concept, we can have wider possibility of coexistence. In addition to that, we have more possibility to coexist with those who we have not coexisted [with before].

That's all I wanted to say. Thank you very much.

[*Applause.*]

Dr. Foreman:

I'd like to thank Mr. Maekawa for such interesting and provocative comments. I am sure there will be commentary following our next presentation, which will be by Professor Kanwar, who will tell you what she is going to be discussing.

Professor Kanwar:

As we are going past morning, perhaps it would be more appropriate to wish you *namaste* instead of good morning. *Namaste* to everybody! After the excellent presentations this morning, I feel very nervous about saying anything because the focus is completely different. Ms. Nathiri had written to me in India, because I don't live here; what she would like to know from me at first hand is how I got interested in Zora and what kind of work is being done about Zora in India, if at all. I must disclaim at the very beginning any expertise or authority. I'm here as a student to learn, and since I come from a post-colonial context, I also very deeply appreciate the significance of Zora's life and work. I think Alice Walker has put it very well, saying that "her work and life project a sense of black people, as complete complex undiminished human beings." I think that is very, very attractive to any oppressed people anywhere in the world.

I'll skip a bit and come to what was my first introduction to Zora Neal Hurston. It was the story "The Gilded Six-Bits" from the *Anthology of American Literature: Realism to the Present,* Volume 2. This is very easily accessible. Before coming here, I went to all the shops in Delhi, book shops—Delhi is culturally quite alive, and the book shops are very good—to see if I could find any books by Zora Neale Hurston, but unfortunately there wasn't even a single book [of hers] on sale. So that puts you in the picture of the kind of access we have to Zora in India. And also the American Center Library, which is a very large library of American literature books in Delhi, had only one single book [by Hurston] and that was "Spunk." That's it. There was nothing else available on Zora.

Now, reading the story "The Gilded Six-Bits" a few years ago, I still remember that I was impressed with the beginning of the story: "It was a Negro yard around a Negro house in a Negro settlement. . . ." Using the technique of repetition, Zora's narrative establishes the rhythm and framework in which the tale is to be told. Instead of taking a black-versus-white perspective, Zora was giving voice to the experience of her own community in relation to itself. Here is the story of an innocent working-class couple, and I'm just summarizing it.

The dark brown Missie Mae and the big tall Joe share an ideal love which is vitiated by the advent of Otis Simmons from "Memphis, Chicago, Jacksonville, Philadelphia," with "his mouth full of gold teethes" and with "rich white man" looks, who introduces the ethic and spurious values of capitalistic America into this very happily ruled Eden. The shattered relationship is restored when Missie Mae presents Joe with a boy child, the spitting image of his father. Motherhood, as we discussed this morning, is valued greatly in third world cultures especially, and here is the qualifier: when the offspring are "normal girl babies to wear our shoes and bring in nothing." Motherhood is valued, but you are a much more valued mother if you produce boys. And in our country, early midwives would just sort of press their thumb to the throat of a little girl and say, "Well, she wasn't alive and she was a still born child." Instead of putting them to the bottom of the lake, as Zora says, they just took the easy way out. And Missy's transgression is forgiven both by Joe and his mother, who resisted this marriage in the first place, as she tells him: "I never thought well of you marrying Missie Mae cause her ma used tuh fan her foot round right smart and Ah been mighty skeered dat Missie Mae wuz gointer git misput on her road."

Well, this aspect seemed similar to my own cultural context, [although] the idiom and the dialect of the characters were very unfamiliar. In order to catch the nuances of the exchanges, I found myself reading the story aloud, so not only did I get the written word on the page, but I heard the voices of the speakers themselves, of course in my own imperfect accent. In addition, here were some expressions and colorful images that I encountered for the first time: "chuckleheaded," "fuzzel duded," "mouth got cross ways," "making feet for shoes," and, of course, something which I was not able to figure out, "fan her foot round right smart," which is a bit of a tongue twister as well. The memorable verbal images are not just restricted to the customary speech of the characters, but to the educated narrator's voice as well: "As Joe rounded the lake on his way home, a lean moon rode the lake in a silver boat. If anybody had asked Joe about the moon on the lake, he would have said he hadn't paid it any attention. But he saw it with his feelings."

So the whole thing is very poetic, the language that Zora uses as an educated person deeply rooted in her community. Zora's double consciousness is dramatized in her use of what Henry Lewis Gates Jr. calls "the two speech communities which are intertwined." This is especially attractive to the educated Indian who speaks the mother tongue at home and English abroad. And despite the oppression that she must have inevitably faced on account of being an African American and a woman, Zora, I quote Sherry Wool, "had created alternative spaces at least in language." This is a familiar strategy employed by Indian writers such as Raja Rao and Moon Kraj Annan, and others. However, within these alternative spaces, white America intrudes. Towards the end of the story, after Joe leaves happily with candy kisses for Missie Mae, the store clerk comments, "Wisht I could be like these darkies. Laughing all the time." For the reader who has shared the suffering, hurt, and heartbreak of Joe and Missie, this strikes a very jarring note and exposes the ideology that structures and maintains stereotypical images in order to maintain, manipulate, and control. And it is these stereotypes, I think, whether in relation to race or gender, that Zora wished to subvert.

This beautifully crafted story was particularly significant for me because it set me off in search of other stories by African American women, the result of which is the book entitled *The Unforgetting Heart: An Anthology of Short Stories by African American Women, 1859-1993*. I don't have a copy to show you. This anthology starts with the first short story published by Frances Harper, called "The Two Offers," and ends with Wanda Coleman's croon in 1993, and it unfolds the whole development of the short story. As it often happens in coming to a literature other than our own, we begin to see our own heritage with fresh eyes. For instance, the human experience rendered in the "Gilded Six-Bits" resonates in a story written by a woman in India. In 1939 Char di Bitchavan wrote "Bonval Shihi," or, literally translated, "Capitalism," a story that recounts the mental agony of the husband, whose name is Guntput, when his low-cost wife, Gajara, is seduced by the rich factory owner. Like Missie, Gajara, too, is faithful in spirit to her husband, but the system and its values make a low-cost woman particularly vulnerable and susceptible to seduction and exploitation.

It is interesting to note this is a story about a Dullet, or a low-cost couple. Now, you might ask, who is a Dullet? The word Dullet literally means oppressed, and it is a name that politically aware Untouchables—you may have heard of them—prefer to give themselves, somewhat in the manner of the term African American instead of more derogatory appellations.

"Untouchable" was a name given to them by their masters for many centuries a denial of identity is a familiar strategy, as we all know, of Apartheid. The lowest in the caste hierarchy — you may be aware that we have a caste system as well — the Untouchable lived in segregation, had no access to education, and was socially and economically exploited. And here in *Jonah's Gourd Vine*, we have Lucy advising her daughter, like all oppressed people that have been denied education, to remember to get all the education she can. "Dat's the onliest way you kin keep out from under people's feet. You always strain tuh be de bell cow, never be de tail uh nothin'."

A similar kind of impulse is to be found in literature by the Dullet community. In the U.S., color is the basic feature of caste, in India it is religion, but in both cases there is segregation in terms of living areas, places of worship, job opportunities. And caste status, as we all know, is something which is determined by birth and is in all societies. The Dullet, or the erstwhile Untouchable woman, has many things in common with her African-American sister. She is oppressed on the basis of her gender, her race, and her caste. Like her African American counterpart, she is in search of a voice and her cultural identity. Dullet writing, too, like Zora's, has its roots in oral culture, folklore, lullabies, and wedding and work songs. Other similarities include the use of nonstandard language and often an autobiographic mode of expression.

Commenting on the parallel of African American and Dullet writing, Dr. Jane Bagmari, a Dullet critic, points out, "The experience of both is based on social and cultural inequality. Both write out of social commitment. The language of both is the language of Cultural Revolution." And these connections have been made way back from the time of W.E.B. Dubois, who, you may be aware, wrote a novel which was published in 1927, *The Dark Princess*. That's the story of a love between an African American man and an Indian Princess. Together, they seek to build the world across the color line. And Zora herself was aware of the situation in India. In her essay "Crazy for This Democracy," she says, "No East Indian may ride first-class in the trains of British-held India. Jim Crow is common in all colonial Africa, Asia," etcetera.

Many Dullet woman writers have yet to be discovered, recognized, and installed in their rightful positions. At a Dullet writers workshop held in New Delhi, Dullet women writers brought massive amounts of notebooks of unpublished creative work. As the work is written for the most part in Miratiqui, Jarati, and other regional languages, it has limited access. Translating it into Hindi or English alone would afford it the visibility that it deserves. Similarly, the majority of Dullet writers who cannot read English will have access to the stories of Zora and other African American writers when translated into Hindi and other regional languages. People somehow have the impression that in India everybody speaks English. That's not true—only 4 percent of the Indian population speaks English—but when you calculate 4 percent of 850 million, that's quite a lot of people speaking English in India.

The short story "Isis," featuring the autobiographical character of the same name, who is later recognizable as Isis Potts in *Jonah's Gourd Vine* and is reintroduced as Persephone in *Dust Tracks on a Road,* has been included in this anthology. I have translated this into Hindi, which will help bring Hurston to an entirely new readership, one that she would no doubt have approved of. This is what Isis looks like in Hindi: (सुलभ कराने). She would be very happy to have her work translated into another language, because in her essay "Art and Such" she's very happy to announce, *"Their Eyes Were Watching God* was published also in England . . . translated into Italian by Ada Prospero and published in Rome." So an international renown was already perhaps burgeoning in the 1930s. Why choose "Isis," all drenched in light, for the anthology translation? Because Isis, surrounded by the chores of ribbon cane and peanut hulls, is able to get on that gate post, look to the horizon, express her creativity in spite of squalid conditions, and—like a creator—jump at the sun.

For Indian women who have centuries of oppression, this image and prospect are especially significant. Since ancient times, the prescribed role for Indian women has been—this is from a sacred law book which prescribed codes of conduct to follow in society, and it says, "Day and night women must be kept in dependence by the male of the families. And if they attach themselves to sensuous enjoyments, they must be kept under one's control. Her father protects in childhood, her husband protects in youth, and her sons protect in old age. A woman is never fit for independence." Within such a context, then, is it surprising that intrigued female colleagues finding a copy of "I Love Myself and I'm Laughing," want to immediately borrow it? For not only would they be borrowing a text, but they would also borrow what Cheryl Wall calls the empowering legacy that Zora's celebration of the self seems to endorse.

This is not to deify Zora, but to read her life and works as challenging the dominant theology of her time, and of showing us not only how to survive and endure but also to prevail. Zora's work is a complex interplay of the very structures of feelings prevalent in her time. In *Their Eyes Were Watching God,* Nanny articulates the dominant ideology: "The nigger woman is the mule of the world so far as I can see." But Janie refuses to internalize what Nanny tries to instill, and Tea Cake is the catalyst who helps her to break out of the colonial mindset and to be free. She will not have the relationships of the oppressors' making imposed on her. As Audrey Lord says, "The true focus of revolutionary change is never merely the oppressive situation which we seek to escape, but that piece of the oppressor which is planted deep within each of us, which knows only the oppressor's tactics, the oppressor's relationships." Janie frees herself not only from the pattern of the oppressor's relationships with Logan Killicks and Jody Starks, but also from conforming to the oppressor's notions of what constitutes womanhood. And, finally, when Janie returns to her community, it is in "dem overalls," a symbol of a chosen class position and womanist ideology. Janie, like Zora Neale Hurston, was born before her time. During the court scene, Janie and the narrator become one as they observe "the twelve strange white men, eight or ten white women, and colored people packed tight like a case of celery." Ultimately, it is her own people who are the most hostile. The scene is strangely prophetic, for it rehearses what is to follow her indictment by black male critics such as Richard Wright, who felt *Their Eyes* "carried no theme, no message, no thought"; and Alain Locke, who recommended that Hurston "come to grips with the motive fiction and social document fiction" rather than create pseudo-primitives.

While motive fiction and social document fiction are now historical curiosities tied to a particular historical moment, Zora still continues to rise. The second incident that so symbolically replicates and acts out the court scene is when the black press indicts Zora for molesting a ten-year-old boy in 1948, effectively undermining her confidence and silencing her for the moment, but not for long. Paradoxically, it's in and through a community that Zora finds her voice. She did not believe in adopting a tone of special pleading for her people, nor in idealizing them. She depicts a people not as types, but, as she says in her essay "Art and Such," as those who "love and hate and fight and play and strive and travel and have a thousand and one interests in life, like other humans."

Hamble says in *Jonah's Gourd Vine*, "You know our people is just like a passel of crabs in a basket. The minute they see one climbing up too high, the rest of them reach up and grab him and pull him back. They ain't gonna let nobody get nowhere if they can help it." Interestingly, this story has some currency in India, and I knew of it before I read Zora. The story is that baskets of crabs were being sported from all over the world, and most of the baskets had lids on them. And there was one basket that didn't have a lid, so the organizers wanted to know what was going on, why this basket had no lid. So they said, "This basket has come from India, and it doesn't need a lid because, if the crabs try to come up, the others will pull him down."

So reading Zora gives me a sense of cultural déjà vu, especially in her references to voodoo. As she herself says, "I learned the routines for making and breaking marriages, driving off and punishing enemies, influencing the minds of judges and juries in favor of clients, killing by remote control, and other things." Now, this is very familiar because I remember growing up as a child in a village [where] this was always below the surface of our daily life. Sometimes we even furtively witnessed spirits being exorcised from people. The local jailer—we call him the witch doctor—would come and first try to beat the spirit out with a broom. If that didn't work, heated tongs were used. So there are so many things which we can sort of relate to in Zora's references to voodoo and other folklore.

While the West has seen third-world voodoo rituals as uncivilized and barbaric, Elliot Butler Evans tells us, "Hurston undermines scientific knowledge by emphasizing subjugated forms of knowledge." No less a personage than Mahatma Gandhi called Western medical science black magic. That was his way of responding to what they were saying about us. In a discussion of Zora's research in this area, I was trying to get female colleagues' response to what Zora was doing, and when we started talking about it everybody came up with their own stories of what they remembered about superstitions and rituals that they were familiar with. What resulted was a modern-day replica of the lying sessions outside Joe Stark's store in Eatonville. And I found that Zora's work has this tremendously dynamic quality of creating a sense of community, because those female colleagues were not necessarily on the best of terms. Zora's introduction to the sub-continent has been recent and is still in its infancy. India has traditionally, because of its long history of British Colonial rule, been a stronghold of English literature. In fact, more people read Shakespeare in India than they do in Britain. American literature is a more recent phenomenon; it was inaugurated in the late 1950s and subsequently buttressed by the power and patronage of the United States Educational Foundation in India, the American Center and American Studies Research Center, which have large libraries. The American literature that has been projected and highlighted has come in two phases, initially the white great tradition of the male stream, featuring the usual greats, Hawthorne, Mark Twain, Whitman, Emerson, Thoreau, Faulkner, Hemingway, followed closely in the margins by the minority male writers tradition, Langston Hughes, Richard Wright, Gene Duman, James Baldwin, Saul Bellow, Isaac Singer, and since then many a dissertation has been written on Herzog and *Native Son*.

Black women writers got visibility only in the 1980s. The film *The Color Purple,* based on Alice Walker's novel, was a major event in popularizing African American women's writing on the sub-continent. Another thing was Gloria Naylor's participation in a seminar on black women's writing. January 1990 was another major event which brought visibility to African American women's writing, and it made *Brewster Place* a much-researched novel. Today African American literature is taught in more than fifty literature departments in India, with Alice Walker, Ann Petry, Gloria Naylor, and Toni Morrison emerging as the favorites among all these people.

In recent past, three doctoral dissertations featuring Zora have been completed as well as some at the Enfield level. In fact, a Ph.D. thesis, *Towards a New Womanhood,* has been published in book form and it focuses on the thematic concerns and visions of Zora Neale Hurston, Ann Petry, and Toni Morrison, placing them within shared tradition. It looks at Hurston as a black feminist writer whose work ushered in a new period of female characters in African American literature and set standards for a new womanhood. In the conclusion we are told that "what sets Hurston apart and demonstrates best the extent of a creative imagination is her blending of folklore with feminism and black self-determination." These concerns are also discernible in some other research titles which focus on Zora. These are in *Racial and Gender Discrimination in Fiction by African American Women. Their Eyes Were Watching God* is discussed, but this is discussed along with several other novels like *Quicksand, The Street, Maud Martha, The Color Purple, The Women of Brewster Place*. In familial characterization in Zora Neale Hurston's "Spunk," the black family is seen as the link in the stories discussed.

Now, you might ask whether there is anything specifically Indian in this response to Zora? Would an Indian response mean looking at text from the point of view of Sanskrit poetics? Or can there be a monolithic Indian sensibility? India, as you know, is a very large country with several cultures and languages. Moreover, the text is grounded in a particular context and carries its own cultural nuances that suggest its own reading practices. Here Zora is helpful because she says, "Nothing that God ever made is the same thing to more than one person. That is natural. There is no single face in nature, because every eye that looks upon it sees it from its own angle. So every man's spice box seasons his own food." Substitute "face" with "text" and we know that the plurality of this discourse is the text embodies are rewritten by the reader's perspective. In that sense Zora's text are, and what is remarkable is that Zora is able to speak to readers across cultures and continents. Barbara Johnson refers to her "multiple agendas and heterogeneous implied readers" and what seems to me as yet another one of Zora's special achievements is that her work, as May Henderson puts it, "speaks as much to the notion of commonality and universalism as it does to the sense of difference and diversity."

Now, the pattern that emerges from the different research topics is, first, rather than focusing solely on Zora, the research places her within a tradition of African American women's writing. Hurston is seen as a literary foremother to Toni Morrison and Alice Walker, due perhaps largely to the popularity of Walker's powerfully moving essay, "Looking for Zora." And this fascination for tracing traditions is rooted in the fact that Indian women critics, understanding the black women's literary tradition, can better understand and recuperate their own. You may be aware of a two-volume book which has come out from the feminist press, entitled *Women Writing in India from 6th Century BC to the Present*. It is one such attempt to bring together the hitherto unknown writings of women from over two-and-a-half million years of Indian history.

Secondly, the research is based mainly on Hurston's short stories and the two main novels, *Jonah's Gourd Vine* and *Their Eyes Were Watching God*, rather than on her white novel, *Seraph on the Suwanee*, or the Afro-Biblical *Moses, Man of the Mountain*. Thirdly, most of the research is carried out by women. In a collection of eleven essays, nine were by women. This could be due to the fact that Zora's work has implications for a redefinition of feminism in relation to our own context. Fourthly, the research focuses on the climatic concerns of race and gender, rather on the more formal theoretical orientations of western critics. That Indian critics have only recently started the race for theory can be attributed to the facts that (a) until recently, theory as we understand it in the age of Post-Modernism had not found a place in literature syllabi; (b) lacking training in the basic concepts of western philosophy theory is largely difficult to comprehend; and (c) however hard one tries to keep up, the average Indian academic always seems to be several years behind what is being produced in the annual American and French traditions.

So people are slightly hesitant of jumping into that particular arena. However, the race for theory has to begin cautiously, for those with the vocabulary and grammar of theory are in danger of setting up the very hierarchies they set out to deconstruct. Reading against the grain of critical theory can often help the subalterns to find the oppositional perspective she needs to articulate her interpretations. Here again Zora has something to say; talking about the African American, she said, "While he lives and moves in the midst of a white civilization, everything he touches is reinterpreted for his own use." In appropriating mimicking and parodying the master's voice, a culturally diverse person can use theory to understand and interpret the play of textual signifiers.

Finally, the research begins on a very, very introductory note often summarizing the plot. As the work of African American women is only beginning to get known, the introduction, I suppose, has become inevitable. It's clear from the connections I have tried to make with the Dullets in relation to Zora's interest in voodoo and her empowering legacy, it's important that her work gets to be better known in India. Last year, 1993, in India, we had plenty of newspaper articles about Toni Morrison, Rita Dowell, and Maya Angelou, for obvious reasons, and people began to know more about African American women's writing, so there's every possibility that Zora Neale Hurston will begin to be better known. But we must try to do something, and this is an agenda I have for when I go back, to see that the books are available in book shops and libraries, inclusion in literature and women's studies courses, exchange of artists, writers, and scholars, and affiliation of American Indian literature associations in India, with a Zora Neale Hurston Society here and the Association to Preserve the Eatonville Community, if it is possible for such networking to be effective across such a distance, and of course translations and comparative studies, but translations, as you know, are contingent upon permissions, and I only have permission for one story which could be published. As for the rest, we will try and see what's going to happen.

Zora has meant different things to different people. She is "funny, irreverent, good looking, sexy," according to Langston Hughes; a perfect darkie to white friends or patrons; a local legend in her community; a native American genius; a genius of the South; a person who could say at one time, "There is no great sorrow dammed up in my soul." And at another time she could also say that a cosmic loneliness was her shadow. And as the shadows disperse, "the cosmic Zora will emerge, one who belongs to no race or time" in her own words, but for all of us and for all time.

Thank you. *[Applause.]*

Dr. Foreman:

I am sure that I absolutely represent the great delight and appreciation [of the audience] to Mr. Mackawa and Professor Kanwar for just absolutely super presentations and provoking thoughtfulness.

Professor Kanwar:

It was out of sheer nervousness; there was no other way.

Dr. Foreman:

It was great! Let's take just a few moments for some questions if there are any that you would like to direct.

Male Audience Member:

The Untouchables that you mentioned—one of the other things that they share with African Americans is they're their own natural group. Isn't it true that the Untouchables are also called, or many of them are called, Obsidian because of their very dark skin they are called black people and that they suffer color prejudice from others?

Professor Kanwar:

Yes, I think that's true, because they were the initial inhabitants of India when the Arians came about thirty-five centuries ago. These people were pushed and segregated, and when the caste system formed, they were the fifth in the caste hierarchy. There are the four castes, the Brahmins or the intellectuals or the upper crust; then you have the Khsatriyas, the warriors; then you have the tradespeople; then you have the Shudras, or people who do the usual menial work for you but are allowed inside the house. The Untouchables were not allowed inside the house, and they had a village outside the village where the caste Hindus lived. Besides that, whenever they came into a town or whenever they came into the village they had to announce their presence by beating a stick. They had to carry a bowl with them so that they wouldn't spit on the ground, and they would spit in that and in the bags. They would often have to tie a broom so that wherever they walked, their footsteps would be swept away. And if somebody was able to touch you, then you would have to get yourself sprinkled with holy water to try to regain your so-called caste.

The Untouchable community has now become very aware of its rights. What you have here is affirmative action; what we have in India is positive discrimination, which means job reservations to the tune of 27 percent. Not enough is filtering down to people who actually deserve it. [Dullets] have always felt a kind of solidarity with the African American people. You might be interested to know that the black bankers here, formed in 1968, had an Indian Dullet bank approved in 1972, and when they made their manifesto they actually acknowledged inspiration from the African American community here. African American women writers have also had a sense of solidarity with the Untouchables in India. For instance, Jane Cortez shared a platform with Dullet poets in New York; J. California Cooper has dedicated her book *The Matter is Life* "To all of you Untouchables in India: you are not untouchable," which I thought was very beautiful.

Dr. Foreman:
Thank you, beautiful.

Tad Hara, Rosen College of Hospitality Management,
University of Central Florida

Woodie King, Jr., 2011 Inductee, Theater Hall of Fame

Cuban salsa singer Celia Cruz backstage

Singer Celia Cruz on stage

Folk art at the Outdoor Festival.

Gospel singer Bobbie Jones

Praise dancer

Valerie Boyd Interviews
Contemporary Artist John Scott

Valerie Boyd is author of the biography Wrapped in Rainbows: The Life of Zora Neale Hurston. *She is an Associate Professor and the Charlayne Hunter-Gault Distinguished Writer-in-Residence at the Grady College of Journalism and Mass Communication at the University of Georgia. Artist John T. Scott, who passed away in 2007, was a sculptor, painter, printmaker, and collagist from New Orleans, Louisiana. Valerie Boyd and John Scott spoke at the eighth annual Zora Neale Hurston Festival of the Arts and Humanities in 1997.*

Valerie Boyd:

I want to tell you a little bit more about this man, unique in all the world. He's been doing art since he started high school.

John Scott:

Since five.

Valerie Boyd:

Well, since five, but you became very conscious of doing art in high school, and it's been a progression, a quest.

Like most jazz improvisationists, he sees life as the past, present, and future all combined. And he is prolific. I have a copy of his resume here, and we're not even going to begin to try and cover it, because he has been exhibiting since the early 1960s, solo exhibitions and group exhibitions. He's been exploring the culture and his philosophy of life as he learns it and interprets and reinterprets it. And I think New Orleans has more public sculptures by him than by any other artist. It's worth a trip to New Orleans just to see them.

He's still a young man; he's still got a lot of work to do. And for that we should all be grateful. He exhibits in a gallery in New Orleans, the Arthur Roger Gallery, and it's in a district that is also worth a trip to New Orleans. It was once an industrial district, and [now it has] galleries and fine restaurants and a hotel I have recently discovered, the Renaissance Arts Hotel. This was evidently built by people who revere art and are major collectors and have the means to be major collectors. From the time you set foot inside the lobby of the hotel, you're in an art gallery or an art world. It also provides space for the galleries in the area to show the works of the artists they handle.

So you can not only enjoy John Scott's work in Arthur Rogers Gallery—which is on Julia Street, a few blocks from the hotel—but you can go to the hotel and see more John Scott as well as other artists in the area. New Orleans is a very creative and energetic place. It's a good place to go to eat and look, just feast your eyes and feast your appetite. I see a lot of smiles out there, so there are obviously people who agree with me.

I had been to New Orleans several times before I met John Scott. When I met him, he was very generous with his time and his vehicle. There were about four of us that he took on a tour of his public sculptures, I should say public monuments. I've been bugging him and his wife to create a map so that people going to New Orleans can receive it and know what treasures are there without having to research or be specialists in the arts field because they are really worthy of a trip. One of the most dramatic, I think, is called *Ocean Song*. I want him to say something about *Ocean Song* before we go any further.

John Scott:
Ocean Song is a mirror finish, stainless steel, sixteen feet tall, with forty-five kinetic elements suspended at the top. When the wind blows, all those elements move. But it's a simple piece based

on a simple idea. We were a people of the wave, and the people of the pyramid—if I'm not mistaken, Egypt was still in Africa this morning. But we are a people that came from the pyramids, over the pyramids, and to the pyramids. What I mean by that is, we came from the continent of the pyramids, and we came over all of those mountains on the bottom of the sea by way of the wave, and if you come to any major city in America, the pyramids are not just a triangular shape any more. They are just as big.

The whole piece is symbolic of that process. I did it in an open competition. The piece was designed and placed on the river in the French Quarter in New Orleans. I was told that the place the piece rests on is the site where Bienville founded the city of New Orleans. I found it very ironic that I won this competition, because here on a site of a city like that is a piece of sculpture by an African American that was commemorative of this whole process. I don't make art about art. To me it's about speaking language. I think art is a language, and public art is a very particular language. I think the artist has a responsibility to the place and the people where that art is going to be placed. That does not mean that I make art that is collaborative, collective, where everybody gets to decide what I make. No, my choice is that I can do it or I can refuse it, but if I'm going to do it, I do it by including people and ideas. I think the greatest thing that I learned in art school was how to listen. It's amazing what you can learn if you listen. And that piece was about many of those things.

Valerie Boyd:

[Another of John Scott's works,] the *Poydras Street Dance: Uptown Second-Line,* captures the movement of a traditional New Orleans brass band parade. The sculpture hangs above the lobby of the 1515 Poydras Office Tower in New Orleans. Before this sculpture was installed in the ceiling, people came in, walked through the lobby, they got on the elevator, they went to an office, they came back down, they walked through the lobby, and they left. Now people hang around there. They feel very comfortable there with all of this wonderful art above their heads, and it's a frequent gathering place.

John Scott:

The "second line" in *Uptown Second-Line* is a part of our history. It came out of the circle dance. The second line basically came out of the black burial society. You got to send somebody off right when they die. You don't just put them in a box and put them in the ground. You got to do it right. And the first line was the hearse, the preacher, the family, and the band. Whenever that would go through, the community, the people that came out of the houses, became the second line because they followed the first line. What's not normally known about that tradition is a Yoruba tradition. The Yoruba people believe that if it rains when they bury you, God is saying you lived a very good life, so when you watch commercials set in New Orleans and see all of those people jumping around with umbrellas, ignore that crap. If you watch a jazz funeral, you'll see that umbrellas do not open until the body is at a respectful distance. Then they make it rain spiritually. So this piece is about the notion of the second line. And in New Orleans anything above Canal Street is uptown; anything below Canal Street is downtown. This is above Canal Street, so it's an uptown segment. It has 76 kinetic elements, each of them ten feet long.

Valerie Boyd:

A Duet for Booker and Fess was done in tribute to two of New Orleans' finest piano players, James Booker and Henry Byrd, also known as Professor Long Hair. The two never played together, therefore the prongs attached to the bow move, but never touch. Very sophisticated ideas are executed in his work. But they are accessible, and that is what is important. Abstraction can be a diversion, so that it is difficult to understand what the artist is saying. But I don't think John Scott is ever trying to trick anybody or belittle the intelligence of anybody in his work. He is really working to make his work accessible, so that all people no matter where they're from can understand it and relate to it.

Now, I think, the most incredible is *Rosa's Stance.* It's a strong portrayal of an African woman representing activist Rosa Parks, whose refusal to give up her bus seat in Montgomery, Alabama, launched the Civil Rights movement in the 1950s and '60s. If you didn't know about that at all, you would know this looks like a woman warrior. And I don't know what Rosa Parks was, if she wasn't a woman warrior. She started a revolution, or she continued a revolution, because it had been started in the rebellions of the slaves earlier.

The man's work is so rich and varied that it's hard to even talk about him in a confined period of time. One of the things that I found so amazing was the wood cut prints of Louis Armstrong. Done with a chainsaw? Those of you who are artists, who know about making art, can just imagine how difficult it must be to take a huge block of wood and cut images and scenes into it, and then make prints on paper from that. But at the Arthur Roger Gallery in New Orleans, I was fortunate enough to see some of those prints. What are the sizes?

John Scott:
Four by eight feet.

Valerie Boyd:
So it's almost like wallpaper. The whole wall is covered. And it's like standing at one end of the street and looking at scenes down toward the end of the street. That's what it was like for me. It was like going back in time to old New Orleans, the New Orleans of Louis Armstrong's time, and seeing scenes, the old wooden framed houses and people standing around or interacting.

And it was done with a chainsaw. If you ever saw anybody use a chainsaw, you'd say that's not possible, but he does the impossible. That's what so exciting about his work. I've never seen prints that are this energetic and this colorful and in this size and scale. The whole gallery was full of these. He works as easily in metal as he does on paper or cutting wood. I just need for him to tell you what he does and how he does it because he works in so many different mediums. And he teaches. If you are lucky and go to Xavier University, he teaches sculpture, modeling, carving in wood and stone, casting in bronze and aluminum, print making. In print making he teaches relief, screen printing, etching, stone lithograph, color graph, design two- and three-dimensional, drawing, paper making, and calligraphy. And if you are ever lucky enough to get a letter from him, it's written in calligraphy. So where does all this energy and all these ideas come from, Mr. Scott?

John Scott:

Well, to say anything about any of this stuff, I should take you back some. I was fortunate enough to go to Xavier University as an undergraduate. I say fortunate because Xavier University was the only university in the United States that had an artist's guild operating when I went there as a student. Those of you that live in Florida, if ever you go to Naples County, go look at the courthouse and the five buildings around it. The sculptures that run around all five buildings, I did as a junior in college. I paid my way through college working as a sculptor—working with master sculptors, the same way they did in Europe. That is how I was trained.

The other thing about the training—and this is extremely important—is that the teachers I was fortunate enough to have taught me that media is like language. If I walked in this room and I could speak seven or eight languages, you would probably think that I was brilliant, but if I walk in a gallery and I can speak seven or eight visual languages extremely well, critics say I am not focused; so strange. The idea of the philosophy behind my work, when I first went to Xavier, a very strange thing took my eye quickly. I noticed when people worked together there, if someone handed another person a tool or an idea and the person said thank you, "you're welcome" was never the response. The response was always, "Pass it on." So the only way you can thank me for something is to give it to somebody else. Well, that's the working philosophy that I operate out of.

This year would be my fortieth year of teaching at Xavier, so I been there a little while. Other ideas about the work—I'll get to the work. You often hear people talk about figuration and abstraction, or reality and abstraction, and I think a lot of time we use those terms and we're not quite sure what they mean, but if you use the African American community as a metaphor, if you think about the blues, the blues is a narrative, it's a story, it's figurative, and if you think about jazz, it's a metaphor, it's abstract, right? But B. B. King and Wynton Marsalis can sit down and play together without missing a note. They can be both figurative and abstract simultaneously. Well, if you're in this language called art, you cannot do figuration without abstraction. That is, you cannot do figuration without understanding abstraction, nor can you do abstraction without understanding figuration. Now, I'll put that in New Orleans terms: in the city of New Orleans, there is an event that takes place that demonstrates that you can have absolute unity and complete diversity simultaneously, without missing a beat. Sounds like a contradiction, right? If ever you go to a second line or a jazz parade, you can have a thousand people in the streets, and they are all dancing to their own thing, but they are all dancing on the exact same beat. Absolute diversity, complete unity—that sounds contradictory, but that kind of philosophy infiltrates what I do.

You know, I refuse to be defined by other people. In 1992 I got lucky and they sent a reporter to my house to interview me for the MacArthur Foundation. The guy came in and sat down and his first comment was "Now that MacArthur has validated you," and I said, "The interview is over. You can leave." The guy didn't know what had happened. I said, "You know, my mother validated me fifty years ago. MacArthur gave me some money. So that whole idea that money validates the art or the artist is a fallacy. It's the paying of the dues, it's the woodshedding, it's learning your craft that makes those things happen."

So, in my art I work in a lot of different mediums all the time. That's not to impress anybody or to show off. I had two musician friends in college teach me a lesson that I've never forgotten. One night these guys used to practice in the studio where I worked in college, and I remember one night the guys came in with a sheet of paper about this long and this high, and it had four lines of music notes on it, and they played for half an hour. And I'm going, "This is the biggest amount of BS I have ever heard. Ain't no way there is that much music on that piece of paper." And they said, "You know, you artists, you find a seed, and you polish the seed. We find a seed, and we plant a tree." I'm going, "That's pretty cool. Explain that." He said, "What we did was, we played these notes forward, then we played them backwards, and then we turned them upside down, played it forwards and backwards. That's four. Then we put it in a mirror and played it forwards and backwards, upside down, forward and backwards. That seed generated eight pieces of music." I've never forgotten that lesson. So when I go into the studio and work on an idea, the idea might end up a set of bronzes, some welded aluminum, some wood cuts, maybe a few water colors, and some prints, and whatever else I can think of, because the more I can surround me with the idea, the closer I can come to telling the truth with that idea.

That leads me into this other thing about philosophy, basically my philosophy in working. I originally referred to it as the J. S. philosophy until a lot of people thought I was being a smarty, and I changed it. I started referring to it as spherical thinking. Now, if you think about that, there are three basic ways that you see people think, if you look at it. One is, most people think like a string of beads in a linear fashion, one idea strung next to the other. Listen to the news every day. If you took one of those beads out, those guys couldn't talk, okay? That's one way. Another way of thinking about ideas is looking at it like it was a surface table: planar thinking, where you can see things that are related on a plane.

About forty years ago, when I got out of graduate school as a young African American, I was really looking for some kind of connection in a continuum between what I was trying to do visually and what I was seeing around me. That being the 1960s, there was a whole kind of conscience-happening in that. I noticed that most of the African American artists I saw were primarily related to something we call the Harlem Renaissance, which was only a blink of an eye in our history. I knew it was a lot more than that. So what I did, I stopped looking at the visual artists and started listening to the musicians, people like Miles Minges, Ray Charles, B. B. King, and what dawned on me was that the continuum of our culture was in the musicians. When we were brought here on those ships, we were no longer allowed to make masks, carve totems, cast bronze, and do the things that once held our history. We could use those crafts, but not for that, right? So the continuum was broken, but the musicians who were given instruments to entertain people at their leisure had the instruments at night, down in the other place. Therefore, they could encode in music that memory. Well, I started studying them, and what I learned was that when you watch a good jazz group perform, three things are always evident. Jazz is always in the now, while you are hearing it, but the musician is also well aware of where they have been—you might call that yesterday, history, the past, and they have an unbelievable anticipation of where they are going, because the notes are not on a piece of paper. That's the future, that's the hope, that's tomorrow.

Well, those guys do all three of those things at one time. That's spherical thinking. So I started working like that. Another way of saying this is, if you can imagine all ideas that was, is, or will be, they are a glass ball and you are suspended in the middle. If you look up, you understand down, because they connect. If you move forward, you understand backward, because they connect. That is spherical thinking. That's what happens in my studio; that's how I work.

Valerie Boyd:

His studio was a warehouse before, and if you see his public sculptures in New Orleans—and I've seen some in Atlanta as well—you know he has to have a huge studio, because he's not working on little things, but *big* things. Well, he works on little

The Spirit House by artist John T. Scott.

things, too, but *The Spirit House*—that's like a house, a small house.

John Scott:

It's nineteen feet by twenty-six feet by sixty feet.

Shadows are extremely important as a part of this piece. The site was chosen on purpose. The whole area was in New Orleans. We have a percent-for-art program, and whenever they do public improvements they have to spend a small portion of money to create art. When this competition opened, we could have chosen any number of sites. We chose that site on purpose. If you look at it from the air, it's a perfect five-point star. The North Star was a compass for black people to find their freedom from slavery, so we chose that spot for that reason.

The reason the house is oriented to the north is that we heard a story that summer. A friend of mine came back through the studio and was telling me a story that he had just heard in Ghana.

During the institution of slavery, people were held at this particular place, and before they were put on slave ships, they were marched around an inside tree nine times to forget who they were. When they went through the gates, they were marched around another tree three times so that when they died their souls would go back to Africa. We designed that facing north so that every morning the shadow of that thing is in the west and every afternoon we send them to the east. So even as the shadows read, it's actually a part of the art.

By the way, for those of you who are in art or think about that stuff, that piece is made out of half-inch marina aluminum, and every last one of those panels was cut by hand in the studio, with a plasma arch and sparks flying. We actually cut the designs out of the metal free hand.

A lot of people see [an art work like *Spirit House*] and treat it like a can of corn. Most young people see a can of corn in a grocery store and it's like the corn appeared on that shelf. Well, somebody had to put it in the ground, fertilize it, keep the bugs away, and grow it. *Spirit House* grew like that in my studio. I was down on the floor with the welding machine—I don't have little dwarves running around doing this stuff. A good friend of mine is a composer by the name of Hannibal Lokumbe. Before *Spirit House* left my studio, Hannibal decided we had to bless the piece in the studio. He picked up some of the cut-outs that were lying around on the floor, and he started playing them, getting sound out of them. So he literally created an instrument by hanging all this stuff. We invited a few friends, put five hundred candles all over this thing, cut the lights out, and Hannibal played this. Then we all left. That used to happen in the studio all the time. An African musician was visiting New Orleans and came into the studio while we were building *Spirit House*. Somebody asked him what was his opinion, and he took out his horn and gave it.

[*Applause.*]

John Scott:

M.J. asked me to tell you about the color. This is a piece of copper in New Orleans, that if left outdoors is going to turn that color, yeah, it's called New Orleans green, but it's actually painted to look like [weathered] copper.

Virginia Boyd:

That's one thing I never liked about the color.

John Scott:

But there were two reasons for that. One is that it's New Orleans green and in color symbology it's also the color of hope. So it's always a double entendre, it's always a double entendre. Word games.

For those young kids in this room who are interested in art, the math, geometry, chemistry, and other courses you take in school—you cannot make art without them. To try and do bronze casting without physics is to create a bomb and kill yourself. So those things are really important, and I say that as one who was mathematically illiterate.

I apologize for this cough. What you are hearing is forty years' worth of scar tissue in my lungs from doing this work over the last fifty-something years.

I forget the date now, but there was a show curated by Rick Powell in Washington, D.C., and Rick invited a number of artists to be in this show. I happened to be lucky enough to be one. He drove me around certain sites in D.C., and he said, "I want you to choose one." As soon as I saw one site, I made a drawing and said, "I want that one." He said "Well, that might be a problem because this is a federal building, and they got some strange rules about what you can and can't do, but I think I can convince them." The piece was called *Blues Migration*. It's a kinetic piece based on a diddlie bow. It has tubes suspended on cables and counterbalanced so that when the wind blows, they have to move sequentially; they cannot move all together. They're painted based on a system called visual mixing. The human eye is the easiest thing to trick; if I juxtapose two colors next to each other, you will see a third color that is not there. These tubes are designed so that as they move, the color relationships change, and you begin to see things that are not there. Anyway, the piece was supposed to stay up for four months. The Smithsonian ended up keeping it for four years. So I guess I convinced them.

In *Street Windows,* as you move around and look through this piece, it actually isolates various parts of a city park in New Orleans. If you look inside the shapes, it's like a picture book that plays with the notion of the park. It's one of the first such pieces I ever did. It's behind the museum in the park, sixteen feet tall, welded steel. I did that one before I had a studio. That was fun.

In 1984 I was asked to be a part of a project, and I ended up as one of the lead designers for the first African American pavilion ever done in the history of the world's fairs. It was called "I Have Known Rivers." The front of the building is covered in words and letters. Martin Peyton and I put every last one of those up by hand individually, and—this isn't a side story for kids—we needed to get all the way to the top of this thing to put words on. We couldn't do it with scaffolding—nobody's arms are that long. So, during the building of the pavilion, I learned how to hotwire a cherry picker. It worked.

I grew up in a part of the city called the Ninth Ward. Those from New Orleans know about that. In 1983, while I was working on the pavilion for the World's Fair, I came across a piece of African mythology that said, when early African hunters would kill something, they experienced a tremendous sense of remorse because they had taken a life. One hunter would hold a bow by the wooden section and change the tension on the string, and a companion would play that string and give a libation of sound to the soul of the animal that gave its flesh to feed the people. Well, the idea so blew me away that I started building shift sculptures shaped like bows and what dawned on me almost immediately is that any line between two points have all the attributes of wave physics—length, frequency, and aptitudes—and if I stick something on the line, I have a kinetic vocabulary. What's really important to me about that is not just the physical existence of it. The fact is, it's the same as the blues. The blues is a combination of African rhythms and western harmonics. [The diddlie bow] is a combination of African mythology and western technology. So I made me a visual blues, and I have been making them ever since.

In *Stony Brook Dance* for the Rugeley Street Station in Boston, each rod is twelve feet long and suspended on cables in the station right across from Northeastern University. When the wind goes through the cable all those things dance.

I was asked to do a piece for a sculpture park in Nashville, Tennessee, so I created a piece called *Tree Poems*. I went through the park and photographed five trees, four standing and one on the ground, and I had the tree shapes cut out of aluminum. I ground them in a special way that they became refractory. To give you an idea of how big this piece, this is only a half-inch-thick aluminum, and when you get to the end of a walking trail, you have to turn right and go up a hill. When you look up that hill, all you see is an aluminum line. You see the edge of these things as you walk up, and as you walk away it turns into a line again. So it's about playing with the human mind. By the way, those things are perfectly flat. All of the reflection stuff on there is done with a grinder.

Five Rings for Philly Joe is in Philadelphia. For those of you who don't know Philly, Joe Jones was an incredible jazz drummer, and when I put up this piece in Philly and told the name of the piece, a couple of people said, "Philly who?" I'm going, "Be for real." Basically, it's a drum set. If you look at any drum set in a jazz setup, you see five drums. So I just took the five drums and turned them into five rings. These things are based on the air conditioning system, so whenever the heat and the air is moving, all the horizontal elements move, so Philly plays every time the heat goes on.

Urban Quartet is in Atlanta, Georgia, behind the Mono towers, twenty-seven feet tall, with seventy-six kinetic elements, each horizontal element six feet long, neo-finished stainless steel and polished granite. Again, you will hear a lot of music terms in my work. With us in New Orleans, we bond with music, you live with music, and you are buried with it.

The only way you can see a piece I did for the Atlanta Airport is to come through customs. It's in the customs area, but it's forty feet across, so the piece is on three different floors. When I was first asked to do this for the airport, I thought about how you travel to Atlanta. If you are up at 35,000 feet and you look down, you can see roads and planning. As you get lower, you see more roads and more infrastructure. As you get near the airport to land, you start seeing buildings and stuff. So the whole thing is a dance of the urban environment.

When I did the gates of the New Orleans museum, I built them so they can open about seven different ways, but when you first open the middle of these gates, all you have left is a pyramid, a triangular pyramid shape. That was done on purpose, because everything inside those gates is derived from neo-classical work, Greek and Roman, and I just wanted to remind people where a lot of that stuff came from.

For the Port Authority building, I did a mural thirteen by feet. It's a simultaneously two- and three-dimensional history of the river. The things you think are three dimensional are flat, and some things you think are flat are three dimensional. I love the contradiction of that stuff.

For the Birmingham Museum I did a piece called *Rainbow Fence and Targets*, about the notion of truth. It has a diagonal line of five hundred glass prisms that are suspended so that every day a rainbow runs across the courtyard and up the side of the building. This piece was built in six weeks with some students in Birmingham.

Ancestral Memory is on Xavier's campus.

At the University of Houston downtown campus is a piece called *Prayer Meeting*. Its little funny shapes have meanings behind them. They reflect the shape of a farm mass, one of the cultures from where we came. They also reflect the shape of a shovel, the reason we were brought here. And they also reflect the shape of a church fan, the spirituality that let us survive. That's what the piece is about. When I was interviewed about doing this piece, the guy said, "What if I said the only way you could get this commission was you had to change the title of the piece? What would you say?" My response was "Call me a cab." I got the commission anyway.

Those of you who are in art will find out very quickly you can get hustled pretty good by some very good hustling people. My sister serves on the Committee for Children, in New Orleans, and they wanted to do a monument in this park. They found out she's my sister, so this was a freebie, done for the organization free. It's twenty-seven feet tall, water jet color aluminum, and it celebrates children at play.

Kansas City at 18th and Vine is kinetic at the top. It's based on the twelve-bar blues that Ellis Marsalis explained to me. So it's the history of 18th and Vine in stainless steel.

This is just an inkling of what I can do.

[*Applause.*]

Valerie Boyd:

I would like to invite you guys to ask questions. The only dumb question is the one you don't ask.

John Scott:

You can ask me anything and if I don't want to answer, I will tell you that too. Come on, don't be bashful. I'm a nice guy.

Attendee:

Would you repeat what you said about the umbrella?

John Scott:

The umbrella that is used in a Jazz funeral is from the Yoruba tribe in West Africa. The Yoruba people believe that if it rains when you are buried, God is smiling on your life and saying that you lived a very fruitful life. When you see a jazz funeral, a real jazz funeral, the people with the umbrellas will not open those umbrellas until the body is at a respectful distance. Then they pop the umbrella open and spiritually make it rain to celebrate the life of the person that is being buried, a handkerchief too. In fact it was a thing among African Americans and I heard this from my mother. I was born in 1940 and my mother told me that her mother told her that when a child was born in the African American community, you cried because they were coming into a life of suffering, and when somebody in the African American community died you partied because they were free. And that's part of our tradition.

Attendee:

My name is Theo McWhite. I grew up here in Eatonville and I'm very proud of that heritage and what I have learned from Eatonville. When we have the Zora Festival, I am always proud to come back and hear the speakers and have my son and my daughter here. My grandfather lived to be one hundred years old, and when you mentioned the umbrella I was just thinking back to his funeral. We were getting ready to put him in the ground when it started raining. I always felt special about my grandfather, who was my mom's dad and he always told a story about when I was two or three. I was very sick as a little baby, I almost died, and my parents were working, and he came home and said, "Why you all haven't rushed this baby to the doctor?" So he took me to the doctor and saved my life. But I've always taken to him, and now that you said that about the umbrella, it means even more to me that I got to spend forty years with him here on earth.

John Scott:

I'll tell you a true story about that. I watched my mother die for a couple of weeks in the hospital, and it's weird because I was being interviewed right after this happened and the reporter was saying how sorry he was, and I said, "You know, for more than fifty years my mother taught me how to live, and in two weeks she taught me how to die, but on the way, my mother had three requests. She wanted to be buried in a pine box, she wanted to be buried with a horse drawn hearse, and she wanted three young priests to say the mass because she knew these guys before they were priests. On the way to the funeral, I explained the umbrella to my sister, who lives in California now, and we were at the mausoleum, burying my mother, when I told her the part about what it means if it rains when they bury you. Lightning struck a tree and it started raining, and to this day my sister won't stand very close to me. True story.

Theo McWhite:

I did see your art work in Naples, which is very nice. [Did you know] you were going to be an artist at five, or when did you think you was going to be an artist?

John Scott:

I don't call myself an artist now. I look at the word "artist" as a word from great old societies. I think it's a very sacred word. You will hear masters in Europe referred to as "maestro," but you will never hear one of them refer to themselves that way. In my lifetime I create something worthy of being called art, my community will call me an artist, but I could never say that. I have been interested in art since I was five years old. My mother taught me how to embroider when I was six, so I still embroider. I have my own hoops and needles. It's funny because she started teaching us that stuff to keep us out of trouble—and if you're sitting on your porch embroidering, and some guy passes by and calls you a sissy, you hop down and go punch the guy out, and then go back and do your needle point. Those are the kinds of things I grew up with. People always made things with their hands, and I assumed everybody did that.

Theo McWhite:

We have a lot of things in common. My mom taught me how to sew at a very early age. I can remember she had her sewing machines. I went to elementary school up to fourth grade before they integrated our school here, but I was in fifth grade when we had to make a pillow and I was the only one in the class who could sew with the needle, who knew how to sew, and everybody said, "How do you know how to do that?" I was always very good with my hands, but I didn't realize I was good in art until I got into high school, until my senior year, in fact. I had Mr. Theodore, who worked with the festival for a lot of years. My guidance counselor told me I had to take an elective, and I had pretty much taken all the electives. He said, "Why don't you take an art class?" Art? I'm not good in art. Well, once I got in there I did a lot of very good pieces. As a matter of fact, I had some things come in first prize in the Winter Park Art Festival. My mom kept a lot of them, but then she gave them to me. I had them stored in my cabinet, and over the Christmas break in my first year of teaching, somebody broke in and stole my paintings. I was heartbroken, but for my son I would like to dabble back into it, because I played college basketball and we didn't realize one of our teammates was good in art. When we were traveling, sometimes we would sketch things and draw things. I think it was 1982 he did a piece that became specialized in *Sports Illustrated,* and that started his career in art. He does very well at it now. Thank you.

John Scott:

My pleasure.

Attendee:

I'm just curious because your art is so full of life and has so much magic and spirit and air and surprise in it. Have you ever had moments, while you were doing a piece, something otherworldly would happen to you?

John Scott:

About forty-five years ago I almost became a Carmelite Monk. This was when I was in college. I almost left and became a monk.

Valerie Boyd:

Would you have continued with your art?

John Scott:

Oh, I'm sure. I mean, I don't *do* art. That's what I *am*.

Valerie Boyd:

So they weren't mutually exclusive.

John Scott:

No, they still aren't. I'm not a very religious person, but I think I'm a very spiritual person.

Valerie Boyd:

I think that's what shows.

John Scott:

I remember having a conversation with a priest a long time ago. In fact, it was an argument. We were talking about prayer, the notion of prayer, and the priest was talking about words and I was talking about something else. I pray every time I go in my studio. The only sad thing is you can't *get* a prayer and because you're visually [oriented] you literally can't *see* it either. Of course, that ended that friendship.

The way that I teach students is that you have to be very serious about doing it. This is not a game. In fact, this is not even a career. It's a way of life. I've had students ask me about earning a living. I don't know how to do that. I know how to live, but I don't know what earning a living means. This stuff is not done nine to five. My third daughter once said, "Dad, I'd really like to get inside your head and see how you think." She thought for a while and said, "Maybe not, so describe what it's like." I said, "Well, if you can imagine a VCR on fast forward and there is no stop button, that's what it's like."

Valerie Boyd:

Like channeling, and we are the beneficiaries. Any more questions?

Attendee:

I just have one question to ask you.

Valerie Boyd:

Tell us your name.

Attendee:

Daniella.

John Scott:

That's sweet.

Daniella:

Thank you. I know there is a lot of symbolism to your art, and I find that very interesting because I do the same thing. I've been doing drawings since I was seven or eight, and everything I do is very symbolic and very detailed. Whenever you do your art, do you come up with more symbolism for it or is it something like you have it all arranged in your head and then you go ahead and put it out?

John Scott:

If I can use this analogy, it's like you just said. You didn't think of any of those words in terms that you had to stop and think what word goes here. You just said them. They just came because you knew the words.

Daniella:

I see what you are saying because the way I have always done my art is, I start with a point and it's not doodling, but everything as I do it is symbolic to what I am trying to get as an outcome.

John Scott:

To me this is a language. Art is not about art, it's about everything else. I have been a very curious person since I was a kid. I read anything and everything I can get my hands on. I've studied calligraphy. A year ago I decided I wanted to make some drawings of flowers, so I went out and bought an encyclopedia on flowers just so I could start reading what flowers are about. I've studied a lot of different cultures and the most common thing in all of them is there are more similarities than differences, so whenever I do work it happens in very strange ways.

I did a series called *The Ritual of Oppressions* in the 1960s. It's a series of bronzes on Rhodesia in South Africa, and it started one morning when I was leaving to go teach. My wife had put some stuff out for Goodwill, and one of the things she had put out was the rubber head of a baby doll. I looked at that head and a phrase popped in my mind: "All of them look alike." Every culture, every ethnic group thinks that people in every other ethnic group all look alike, right? And I thought all baby dolls look alike, so I took this rubber baby doll and made a mold that I used for about 40 different pieces, and even though it's the same head, none of them look alike. Seeing that baby doll head transformed a whole bunch of ideas. It's the circle. If I see one dot on the surface of that ball, I see all of them.

When I think about my work, I don't think about a subject and say, "Oh, let's see how I can do that." Normally, when an idea comes to me, it comes like it's wrapped in a package. It's there. There's a story about Miles Davis—when they did "Bitches Brew," Miles walked in and handed out a whole bunch of sheet of music and there was no music on it and the guys were going, "What?" The idea was "Trust me enough to follow me." When I go into the studio and start dealing with an idea, it's like those blank sheets of paper. Playing with all that metal and all the paint and the other stuff is when the notes start happening and the music builds itself. I don't know any other way to explain it.

Daniella:
That makes perfect sense.

John Scott:
Good, I'm glad.

Valerie Boyd:

Any more questions or comments?

Attendee:

Who are some of your favorites? I don't want to call artists "maestros."

John Scott:

How much time you got?

Attendee:

You can't say your top three?

John Scott:

Let's see, Indian culture, Asian, Tibetan culture, African American culture, European culture and a few others.

When I first started studying this stuff, anything that had ever been done by a human being trying to express themselves in a visual form—that was mine. That's the encyclopedia out of which I get my words. So there are a lot of artists that have influenced me whose names I have never known. I was asked to do three pieces for a church—an altar, a lectern, and a priest's chair—and I did this work similar to *Spirit House*. When I did the priest's chair, I wanted to put on the back of the chair: Matthew, Mark, Luke, and John—the four evangelists. The calligraphy that I used was based on the graffiti I saw on the wall in the city. I took that design and put it in the back of the chair, the priest's chair. Why not? Young people go to church too. I find inspiration all over the place. Folk will say that's "classical" or "folk," but I don't make that kind of separation.

Attendee:

What's the longest you've ever spent researching for a particular piece?

John Scott:

Remember when those four little girls got killed in Birmingham? I'm still doing that piece. I've done one in Orlando, over at the Graphics Workshop. I was a guest down here years ago, and I did a piece, a series of glass prints on that subject. Right now in my studio I'm still working on it. One of these days I'm going to get it right.

Attendee:

I'm one of the few women who visit areas and go to the museums instead of going shopping and other places. I've seen a lot of art work, what I have seen tonight is spectacular. The other day I was watching television and I saw one of the elected officials talk about saving social security by no longer giving money to the arts. I was so distressed to hear that.

John Scott:

That's going to happen unless people like you decide it's not going to happen.

Attendee:

I know that we don't give enough money to the arts, but do you think we are going to lose the little that is coming?

John Scott:

I think the easiest thing in this country to attack is the arts, because there are not that many collective spokesmen for it. Most of the people that attack the arts are like a dog attacking a hub cap on a car. Even if they caught it they wouldn't know what to do with the car. The other thing is, this is a very young country. Think about how young the United States is. In cultures like China with the Great Wall; Egypt; cultures in Africa, Thailand, Tibet; Native American, people have a respect for culture because that is what binds them as a people. Until the United States understands that the culture of this country is not a blanket, but a quilt, we will never appreciate it. Until we accept the fact that we live in a multicultural society, it's not going to happen. The thing is, the sad thing about us is, we are a quilt and there are a lot of holes in the quilt because we haven't accepted those patches yet. Maybe someday.

Valerie Boyd:

Will you tell us a little bit about the uniqueness of Xavier University and why you have spent so much of your life there as a student and as a professor and as a head of a department?

John Scott:

I went to Xavier University as an undergraduate. I respected the place and I never in my life intended to teach in anybody's university anywhere. All I wanted to be was an artist, whatever that means, but my mentors asked me to come back and teach at Xavier for a couple of years. I went back and said, "I'll give you two years and then I'm out of here." That was forty years ago. One reason for that is, in forty years of teaching, all I've learned is how much I don't know. So if I stay there a little longer maybe I'll learn something. The other reason is, I got tired of hearing people say that those who can, do, and those who can't, teach. I will put what I do against anybody on the face of this planet and I intend to win. And that's the attitude I try to teach young people.

I was a basketball player too. In fact, I turned down a college scholarship for basketball to make art. They thought I was crazy, but I can make art till I die. I can't play ball that long. To me, basketball was always a game, not a profession, and I played until I was forty. I used to play in the summer leagues.

But the idea was that if you are going to do this and you do it well, you are obligated to pass it on to other people. Every great artist you can think of in the history book taught somebody. Can you imagine the worst thing in the world being that you have this stuff inside of you and you die before you can give it to somebody else? That's the most frightening thing in the world. You have this incredible thing inside you and you are so selfish that you don't give it away.

One last comment: when my oldest daughter was born, I was in the hospital, and the first time I saw her was through the glass window in this hospital. I nicknamed her The Butterfly, and for a very obvious reason. The only way you can ever hold a butterfly is to never close your hand; if you do, you kill it. The only way you can love a child is to never close your hand. They can leave, but they can come back. And the only way you can ever have an idea is to share it, because if you close your hand, you're going to kill it. That's why I teach.

Artist John Scott

Hurston biographer Valerie Boyd

Step dancers

Celebration!

Actor Robert Hooks

The Ramsey Lewis Trio

White Face dancers

Morris Day and the Time

A Presentation from Poet, Essayist, and Lecturer Nikki Giovanni

Nikki Giovanni is a writer, activist, and educator. She is a Distinguished Professor of English at Virginia Tech. Giovanni has written more than two dozen books including volumes of poetry, collections of essays, and children's books. Her books of poetry include Black Feeling, Black Talk, *and* Black Judgment. *Giovanni spoke at the twelfth annual Zora Neale Hurston Festival of the Arts and Humanities in 2001.*

N.Y. Nathiri:

Good evening. We are about to start the program so, if you will, find your seats, please.

Sybil Pritchard:

Good evening. I'm Sybil Pritchard and I'm a member of the PEC board and I have been asked to welcome you tonight. Thank you so much for coming. We hope you will all take part in all the festivities this weekend.

We have a very exciting program for you tonight and I know you'll enjoy it. So I will call on the next person, Douglas Roth, the interim principal. Is he here tonight? No? Okay, is there a sponsor for Universal in the audience? No? N.Y., do you want to do that?

And, again, we really appreciate your taking part in this tonight and we know that the rest of the program will be wonderful and the three days of activities, as you know from the programs that you have, are going on and particularly the Festival on Saturday, so please try and be there. Thank you.

N.Y. Nathiri:

On behalf of Universal Orlando I want to welcome you here and I want to take a few minutes to talk about the quality of partnership that Universal Orlando has committed to as a part of the Zora Neale Hurston Festival of Arts and Humanities. Universal Orlando is a presenting partner for the educational activities that are taking place today and tomorrow as a part of what is called the Young Voices Conference. The Young Voices Conference is about 100 high school students in grades 9-12. These are particularly interested and strong readers; also students who are enrolled in advanced placement, international baccalaureate, and honors programs.

We are very proud to have the opportunity to present this pre-festival conference today for young people because part of cultural preservation is passing to the next generation those literary and humanities ideas that are so important for a strong and healthy culture. Universal Orlando has sponsored that presentation by Ms. (Nikki) Giovanni as well as the Education Day programs that are taking place on Friday the 26th of January.

Additional sponsors are Orange County Public Schools, the State of Florida Division of Cultural Affairs, The Florida Arts Council, Orange County Government, and United Arts. These are the organizations that have helped to make this program tonight free and open to the public. Thank you very much.

Dr. Jerry W. Ward, Jr.:

I've been given the delightful task of introducing Nikki Giovanni. Fortunately part of that has been done. In the programs you were given, there is a very interesting introduction that gives you all the facts. Now, in the Hurston tradition, I want to give you all the lies.

You know that we have American poets who are national treasures, and for those people, a certain cliché does work: this person needs no introduction. Unless the American people have been, as I like to put it, playing some kind of three-dimensional chess with some variety of Rip Van Winkle, everyone in America knows who Nikki Giovanni is. If you don't, then I'm going to pray for you. People like poets, or they tolerate them, or they dislike them with a passion. I mean they are no holds barred. Nikki Giovanni is a person who has gotten mixed responses, but most of us like her. And some of us love her.

So, as a woman who came of age around the same time I did in the 1960s, I'd like to say she came of age at a time when politics was not a game that one could play by asking, "Was Chad pregnant or was he hanging?" Then when you think about it, a pregnant male? Well, anyway, that's Florida politics. She understood politics when it was a matter of life and death; truly, not figuratively, but literally a matter of life and death. She's always had to temper her black talk and her black judgment with a sometimes plain and a sometimes Godiva-chocolate-sophisticated sense of humor.

I want you to note that humor is not a synonym for what is funny. Indeed, at one point in the English language, humor referred to a constituent feature of the human body. So let that be a warning because, like Langston Hughes, Nikki Giovanni has mirrored the simple, very fundamental, aspects of her readers' lives and thus given them something to think about; something that needs as much chewing as a piece of sugar cane.

On behalf of the Young Voices Conference and the 12th Annual Zora Neale Hurston Festival, I wish to welcome Nikki Giovanni to Zora's home place and yield the stage to her. Perhaps she will entertain us and enlighten us and tell us the answer to an agonizing question that I have. Why, from her poet's angle, is truth, like salvation, always on the way?

Nikki Giovanni.

Nikki Giovanni:
Whose is this? Relatively low maintenance. We have been working on getting things - here we go - together. There we go. [Trying to raise the music stand with her notes on it]. I was totally excited - there must be a screw, isn't there a screw? What is life without a screw? This is why I don't get invited back. I was totally

excited to be invited to the Zora Neale Hurston Festival. There is a screw, isn't there? [Continuing to adjust the stand] I was going to bring it to eye level.

That's the only thing about growing old and I'm a big fan of growing old. I recommend it, I really do. A lot of people don't get to be old. I'm a Virginian so I'm not laughing at you Floridians but, you know, a lot of people in your state are legally blind who are on the road. They are, and they always have a driver's license from Ohio. And they kill all these people and they say, "Gosh, I didn't see them." "Well, no, actually you are blind, sir, and your children shouldn't let you out." But we're not frequently able to control...

I'm very proud of my mother and I shouldn't start things this way, should I? But I am very proud of my mother who is 82 because ten years ago she quit driving and I told her that I'm really happy because, of course, people don't. That's a whole other discussion, I know. People don't quit driving because we don't have public transportation, and you don't have any other way to get around, and yet you and I pay taxes and whatever it is we are doing with the taxes is not helping people get around because we have legally blind people having to drive. So something's wrong with that and, of course, now...

I said to myself I'm not coming to Florida and make any bad jokes, 'cause I'm not, but, you know, I think it's Al Gore's fault and I'm a registered Democrat. I voted Green, I voted for Nader because I figured the Greens are right and we got to save the Everglades, but Gore was arrogant and Gore decided that he didn't want to be bothered with Bill Clinton, he didn't want to ask Clinton diddly. But everybody, and this is not Nikki doing Democrat publicity, I'll just do it quickly because it makes me crazy. But he didn't want to ask Clinton for help because Clinton, you know, had sex with what's her name? Monica, right? She was alive. I mean, I could see it if she was dead; the president having sex with a dead girl is unattractive.

See, what I mean, I don't want to identify with somebody who is screwing some dead woman, that's not good. But she was alive and she was grown and I get so sick of people acting like a grown man and a grown woman had done something that grown men and grown women didn't do, and then they turn around and say, "Oh, but you know he's married."

But I know one thing... he's not married to me. That's between him and Hillary and somebody got mad at me and said, "What about Chelsea?" I said, "Chelsea's a child." That's the truth. Nothing makes me angrier than children bothering with adults' business. Chelsea is supposed to shut her mouth and go back to Stanford and graduate. 'Cause it had nothing to do with Chelsea. Nobody ever had sex with somebody else and said, "I wonder what my daughter's gonna think." I don't think so.

Chelsea needs to suck it up and go on about her business and I would say the same thing if any of you in here, your parents are not together, it is none of your business. They are grown and you are not, and they are still both your parents, so get over it, get used to it, and smile at both of them and go on about your business. Anything else is going to make you crazy. And you gonna find yourself at 50 wondering what happened to your life, you mad at two people who are now good friends.

I was sick about Gore because I live in a state, I live in Blacksburg, Virginia, Virginia Tech, and we actually went 11 and 1 this season. *We* should have played for the national championship, but there's some state someplace that has some team that the quarterback is older than a third of all of the NFL quarterbacks.

Mr. [Chris] Weinke is going to graduate from college [Florida State University] and collect Social Security. I couldn't believe it, and then Bobby Bowden, you know they talk about power, Bobby goes just gets him [Weinke] a Heisman. How the hell did he win a Heisman when there's Josh Heupel over at Oklahoma who took his team 12 and 0? I know I'm in Florida but give me a break!

That kid - but that's not what we started off talking about. I just wanted to mention this because I live in Blacksburg and Blacksburg is only 90 miles from Lynchburg and Lynchburg is the home of Jerry Falwell. You all remember Jerry because we all had to hear about Jerry, and I get so sick of ... see, I'm not going to stand up here and tell you that I'm a Bible scholar because I'm not a Bible scholar. I just know what I know from Sunday school and from the hymns that I listen to and stuff like that.

But everybody was upset. I'm just mentioning about Bill 'cause I'm tired of it, you see. And it's not that I'm just tired about Bill 'cause Bill's gone. I'm tired of the whole sex trip. It's time for that to be over. And everybody was bitching and moaning because Bill did this and Bill did that, and you say, "What's the problem?" "Well, he was unfaithful, and he committed adultery, yak, yak, yak."

And I said, "Yeah, but didn't David sin?" I mean, I know I'm not a Bible scholar, but didn't David send the husband of the woman that he wanted to the front line, thereby guaranteeing he would get...? I mean, I remember David a little bit. And it seems like David was a fine leader except for this small flaw about wanting that woman. Didn't Solomon do something very similar?

So it's very funny to me unless I say I don't know my Bible. I just remember a couple of these stories sometimes, and all the born again Christians, I don't know what Bible they read, but they're not reading the Bible I'm reading because seems like I remember some of these stories about some of these people and God didn't turn his back on them. He recognized that we just people and we're stupid and we make the same mistakes over and over again. And it's time to get beyond this stuff but I'm tired of the whole sex trip.

I just wanna, I do want to mention that, because what we have done right now, and it may swing back again, but what we have done right now is substituted sex for race. So every time now the little crazy white boys wanna go around and kill somebody, in the old days what they would do, and it's only fair, I'm not picking on anybody, I'm in a good mood, I am, but there is a history here.

What they used to do in the old days is they would find a black boy walking down the road or whatever and they would lynch him or castrate him - whatever they were feeling like doing that day. Nobody does that anymore because it is so unattractive. Every now and then in Texas you'll find somebody dragging somebody behind but, the thing is, it's very unattractive, it's very embarrassing, but they do it, you understand what I am saying? And then we have to execute them, and that's embarrassing 'cause nobody wants to live in a country that executes people. All of that is really bad.

But what they do now is they beat them to death, and they say, "Why did you do?" "Sir, he was gay." That's what they say and honestly the black community cannot be in total sympathy with the gay community because it's exactly what they do; they beat them to death because they are gay.

Somebody said, "Well, I don't like gays." Well, you don't have to like gays, they didn't ask you to like gays, all you have to do is not murder them because it's so unattractive. It causes so many problems, makes everybody feel bad. Somebody said, "Well, he made a pass at me." Well, it's a good thing that women don't kill men every time; there would be a lot of dead men. "So, what happened, he told me to come by his house later." Boom! What kind of sense does that make?

What it is, we got an excuse for hatred and that's not a good idea. We have to grow up. It's the 21st century. Somebody say, "Nikki, you asking me to tolerate it?" No, I'm not. I'm not asking you to tolerate, I'm not asking you to do anything. I'm asking you to tend to your business. That's all - if you don't want it, don't deal with it.

There's a lot of things people don't do. I don't smoke anymore. I'm not trying to stop anybody from smoking. I'm just trying to stop you from smoking around me. I had a cancer. I do not recommend cancer, so if you're young and you don't smoke, I'm gonna say, don't do that. I had a cancer in my left lung. And it's a very frightening thing and I think one of the really not good things to hear.

My doctor is a cool guy; his name is Kenneth. Kenneth is very cool. And Kenneth said, 'cause I was having a lot of trouble, my blood pressure was up and my hand hurts a lot of the time, I'm trying to write a book about it. And Kenneth is one of those people like, "I don't know what's the matter." He said, "Why don't we take an X-ray?"

So I said, "Take an x-ray," because I just know I wasn't feeling good. So he takes an x-ray and he's one of those people like "Nik, why don't you ...?" He calls me Nik. "Nik, why don't you come look at this?" And I said, "Kenneth I don't want to." You know, you hear the voice, "I don't want to look at this, you're the doctor."

"You don't want to look at this, so you should." I said, "Kenneth, what are you saying?" "Well, there's this mass." I said, "Oh." He said, "It doesn't have to be cancer." Yes, it is, 'cause I'm colored, I'm a woman, I am not lucky. No, all of them things together just means it's cancer. If I had been white, or I had been a man, maybe there would be a chance, but me, it's cancer.

"Well, I don't know if it's operable." Oh, Kenneth, it's operable, and I knew that. It's operable because I'm a believer in cuticle scissors, and if I had to stand, I am, and if I had to sit there and cut, it's coming out. It has to come out. You don't want anyone tell you the tumor you have is not operable.

The question is, will I survive the operation? And so that's what I was hoping. My mother said, "Well, I'm really worried. I'm gonna come with you." I had to go to the hospital. I said, "Don't come with me." And that's the truth. I said, "Don't come with me."

'Cause there is one thing I know, and it took her a while to understand, there is one thing I know, my mother would have taken the cancer for me. If it was up to my mother, you see what I am saying, I would live forever 'cause your mother is always there whatever it is. I said. "No, because if I have to worry about you sitting up in a hospital worrying that I'm not going to get well... So why don't you stay home, drink a beer" (that's true 'cuz she drinks beer and I knew that would make her feel better) "watch the games."

And, of course, mothers do that wonderful thing. I said, "You talk to that man that you talk to when you worry and let's see what we can do, so if he can't make me well, he can make you feel better." And that's the truth 'cause I was in the hospital almost a month, and that's why, and I don't want you to think I'm here complaining, I just want to share this, this is why I hate people who work for the HMOs. And if any of you work for the HMOs, don't tell me, because I hate them.

Because, I'm in the hospital, they have taken my left lung out; they do that from the back so my back is split open. It's February the 4th, can you imagine, I'm in Cincinnati Ohio, how cold it is. There is ice out there and my HMO (and I paid what they asked me to pay; this is not, "Call us up and tell us, you name your price.com"). I paid what they said: "If you pay this every month when you get sick, we will let you stay in the hospital until you can be well." I did what I was asked to do.

I then got sick. It wasn't like I said to myself, "Hmm, I can make a lot of money if I would go in a hospital and take my lung and I could lay around for a couple of days and really enjoy it!" No, I was sick; it's not going to get much sicker than what I was.

They said, "She been in the hospital four days, we're not going to pay anymore." And I'm very fortunate. You know what happened? This is exactly... I'm very fortunate my attorney is crazy. They didn't know that, but they found it out. No, Gloria is not well, that's the truth. I've always loved her for that 'cause I always knew that it didn't take a whole lot to make her go off

And she totally went off, she was threatening to sue them, their mother, their unborn children, she did everything, and so they finally said, "Oh, let her stay." It was not a favor to me. The favor to me was that I was trying to get well. "Let her stay" did not do it.

Do you know that people die in America? Do you know there is somebody right now having a cancer, having breast cancer, having a vaginal cancer, having a cervical cancer, there's some woman someplace that doesn't have a crazy attorney, and we got that fool sitting in Washington DC and he's not even thinking about it. I really dislike the Bushes, and I'm sorry about that because it's not good to dislike people.

It's crazy; we need universal health care; we need to take care of people. I live in a state that, for probably about every 100,000 persons there is a doctor. I live on the other side, I don't live on the Washington side, I live in the mountains. We don't have hospitals and we don't have doctors and we don't have kids who get vaccinations. So people still die of measles, how do you explain that in 2001, how do you explain people dying of measles?

People still, old people, still have to make a decision on whether or not they can afford prescription medicine. They didn't wake up in the morning and say, "I think I will take five pills today." Their doctor said, "This is what keeps you alive." They have to choose between that and food, between that and heat and everybody says it's okay? It's not okay, and America needs to do better, they need to get over it and they need to do better.

We have a lot of rich people in America and they are going to be rich. I know Jesus, speaking of Jesus, he said, "The poor will always be with you." He missed it. I'm not arguing with Jesus but he missed it. It's not the poor who are always with us, it's the rich because the poor you can get along with, it's the rich that are crazy. They have everything and then they want everything and they don't want to pay taxes for it.

Bill Gates wants to be the richest man in the world. What the hell does that mean? He is still richer than you and me at ten million dollars. I can't even aspire to that but he wants billions so he can do what, buy a house, buy a car, buy food, get cashmere diapers to his children? What does he want to do that he needs billions of dollars so that other people sleep out in our streets, so that other people are hungry, so that other people have to open up dog food that they then mix up in the gravy so that their kids won't know what they're eating because they are trying to feed them and you know what happens and so do I.

Something's wrong with that; we need to tax those people. If you don't want to be taxed, be poor. That will solve it. I live in a state that has something called a car tax. My car is fourteen years old; I like the car. I have a job, they'd sell me a new car. I like the car I have. I drive a MR2, a 1987 MR2. It's nice - it's a little red car and it's my favorite, and I like it and I keep it and I pay whatever it is I'm supposed to pay, and we have a tax and it's called a car tax, you pay on it according to the worth of your car. So if you want to buy a Lexus, you wanna buy a Jaguar, you wanna buy a BMW, then if you can buy an $80,000 car, then you can pay tax on it. But all the people with the $80,000 car said, "Well, if I pay all the taxes, I won't have any money left over.

Get a life. I just thought I would mention that. 'Cuz you get sick of it and we living in a time where we could make better decisions. I 'm just a poet, I came here to read poetry. I did, but you get sick of it, and I think sometimes somebody needs to remind us that we are not crazy when we are sick of it. We can do something better than what we see. I know we can.

This whole human question is still an experiment that nobody's quite sure it is working. I think it ought to work. I basically think human beings have a potential and I know that everything (you know this, too) there's a clock ticking on everything on earth. And I'm not picking on the conservatives but, you know, conservatives are always like, you know, well, an extinct species. You know, things run out. There's a clock ticking on us too and one day human beings will be gone.

It's the truth, and I know we don't like to think about it like that 'cuz we are human beings, but we are a mess. So nobody's gonna miss us; that's what bothers me. I say that to my students all the time. If tomorrow there was a question, "Should human beings continue?" who would speak for us?

Maybe the domestic dog. I think the dog essentially likes us. I think that if there was a caucus going on, the dog might; air wouldn't, water wouldn't. I can't think of one species of bird that would say, "Yeah, let them stay here." I can't think of, I can't, who would speak for us? Not the Florida panther, not the alligators. Who would speak for us? Maybe the silverfish 'cause they live in our books, maybe the roaches because they live so close to us. Who would speak for us?

Even we, even we, if it was us and God said, "Should we continue?," even we would be hard pressed to say, "Sure." We would have to say not, "Certainly," but, "Have mercy." We would have to say, "Please". We would have to ask for another chance.

We can do better than this; we can move this experiment forward. We can have something to be proud of when it's over. It's what we say to youngsters about leading their lives. We try to tell them, "You have to lead a good life because at the end you want to be able to look at yourself and say..."

I don't think about it that way. That's what it's all about and the species is the same thing and it's not about screwing, and it's not about drinking, and it's not about gambling, it's about who you are and what you've tried to do. And about those superficial things that come up that people try to make some kind of sin or some kind of ... it has nothing to do with it. It has to do with who we reached out to help. It has to do with how we stood up for something.

And when this earth - and it will be finished at some point. I'm a big Star Trek fan. You remember the Star Trek 2, the planet disappeared and Solo, ah, Sulu, was having his own starship and all of a sudden the starship is shaking and they realized they were by a planet that dissolved and so he goes, "Computer, what was that?" And they said, "It blew up." It was a planet that blew up and nothing was left but the energy.

I'm a big fan of black holes 'cause they're black and they're not a hole. That's a whole 'nother discussion. But they're energy and at some point, when this planet is gone, the energy of this planet will continue in the universe. And wouldn't it be a wonderful thing if, when the space ships go sailing by in 5000 and 6001, they go sailing by and ship shakes, and somebody says,

"What is that?" And they said, "It was earth," and the people sitting there felt the love, felt the courage, felt the hope, and said, "These must be great people. I feel their energy."

You and I know that and somebody could say, "Yeah, Earth was composed of a lot of people, black, white, brown, and yellow. They tried to get along; they tried to build a society; they tried to live with other life forms; they did the best that they could." Wouldn't it be a wonderful thing to know that we could be remembered for the beauty that we are and not the craziness that we keep perpetuating? So I just wanted to mention that because we ought to be proud of this time that we spend in this form on this planet in this universe. It shouldn't be asking too much that life be a good thing. That life be something that brings us joy. That's what I think.

But I came to read poetry. I really am a big fan of black women, and that's not that I'm not a fan of other women, but I'm a big fan of black women. And *Essence* magazine had their 30th anniversary (actually, I couldn't believe *Essence* had their 30th anniversary) last May, and I have a son.

I don't know if any of you have children, I think children are okay, it's just, I mean, I wouldn't take anything away from my son, I like him okay, but you do get tired of them. If anybody ever tell you they don't get tired of their children, either is on drugs or don't know their children. That's the truth.

But I did for my son what I could, what I thought I should. Actually, my mother sent me to school. I sent my son to school and I was very happy my kid graduated from Morehouse, and it was like, "Aww," and you go and you cry and you're just so delighted.

And then he says, because we had a graduation dinner, and he says, "Mom, I was thinking about going to law school." And I said, "That's wonderful," 'cause you always want to think about your kid in a profession. And I thought, "Yeah, that's wonderful, and you know you can use my home as your address. And your loan applications, I'll send them right to you." And, you know, I was being positive.

And I have a friend and he said to me, "You know, Nikki, you can't do that." I said, "I can't do what?" He said, "You can't let Thomas get a bunch of loans" (my son's name is Thomas) he said, "because he gets the loans, he goes to law school, and he's gonna come out in '70 to $100,000 worth of debt. He's gonna get a job, something's gonna go wrong. They're going to hand him the piece of paper, tell him to take it down to Wall Street, he's gonna be the kid because he's the low man on the totem pole, he's the black kid in the law firm. He's gonna get arrested for insider trading or something, he's gonna go to jail, lose his license. You know that's what happens to little black boys who do things like that, and they have to 'cause they have the loan to pay off." He said, "He'll be in jail. You'll be visiting him in jail, and it will cost you as much money to go up and visit him in jail, so why don't you send him to law school?"

I said, "Thomas has been talking to you, hasn't he?" But I try to do the right thing because my mother would have done it, and that's what she said, "That's what I would have done had he been my son." I said, "Mom, I didn't go to law school."

But, never mind, I sent the kid to law school. Any of you sent your kid to law school? So you have an idea of how long and how arduous this is. But I was happy because I have a kid, and he did graduate from Georgetown Law, and I went and I cried and I was so happy for him. I did, and he got a job, and I was so happy about that.

And, I don't know if this happens to you, but it happened to me; like he graduated in May, and at the end of June there was money left over in my checking account. You know how you get your statement from the bank and there was money left over. And I thought, something's wrong here, so I called the bank. "Hi, it's Nikki Giovanni, and whatever my numbers are, and there's some mistake, there's a positive balance. I mean I haven't had a positive balance since he was in high school.

And they were like "Oh no, Miss Giovanni, it's money." But I know, you know, the bank makes a mistake, and you spend the money and then you have to pay it back. I'm not falling for that; they made a mistake and they will find it out, you know.

But then July, there was money left over, and then September, so I went to the bank, sat down with the Vice President, and said, "You all have to stop this because it's throwing my…, I can't keep track of my books, I'm having money left over."

Because I'm one of those people, you write a check on Thursday hoping you can get to the bank on Monday before it hits. 'Cause you got a kid in law school, you doing things.

And it's like "No, Miss Giovanni, that's your money." I said, "How did that happen?" And it's just one of those things where I look in my pocket and it's, "Oh, Thomas isn't in my pocket anymore."

So I did something that I hadn't been able to do in like 25 years; I took a vacation. It's like I'm gonna take a cruise, which I was so thrilled about. Now, I don't know when *you* get ready to take a vacation how *you* do it, but it's like September. I teach at Tech and we have the long break, so it's like December and I'm cruising the Panama Canal because always wanted to go to the Panama Canal. And it was 2000 and the Panama Canal was being returned to Panama, which it should be.

I was excited to go to the Panama Canal because I am a big fan of Marcus Garvey. We all know Marcus Garvey. But the reason we know Marcus Garvey, as you well know, is Marcus Garvey's family ran a newspaper in Jamaica because the most people that got killed on the Panama Canal was, you know, Jamaicans.

And so many Jamaicans were dying that Marcus Garvey went over to find out, he spent time in Costa Rica and then he spent time in the Canal Zone, to find out why the Jamaicans were dying. And they were dying because the Canal was abusive, as you well know.

And he went back and he wrote that up in his newspaper and they published it. And the British (and I like the British) but the British were a little bit upset about what Marcus Garvey's family was publishing. And so they did what people do when they don't like what people say, because it's all about what people say. And so they went to Marcus's family and, most of you know this history, and they said to Marcus's family, "Here are your choices, boy. You can go someplace or we are going to kill you." And one of the things you like about the British is they are real clear, so there was no, I wonder what they meant?

And so his daddy called him in, and you know these things, and said, "Marcus, they're going to kill you if you keep writing. Where would you like to go, son?" And we would do the same thing for our children.

And Marcus said, "I have always wanted to meet Booker T. Washington because I would really like to start an institute like Tuskegee Institute in Jamaica." They said, "Well, go on, we'll send you."

They put him on a ship to send him to New York, which is where he got, but when he got to New York, Booker T. had died. As you well know, and since Booker T. had died, he never left Harlem but, in fact, started the United Negro Improvement Association which was, and still is, the biggest gathering of Black people in a single organization. Now we know that [W. E. B.] DuBois didn't like it, and James Weldon Johnson, but this is not what I was saying.

I just thought I should go to Panama Canal, and I thought I should go because we were giving it back over, and I was very proud of all of the history of all of the black people who built that canal. I did what anybody else would do going to the Panama Canal; I called the President.

Well, I figured he was going, right? It was Clinton, so I called. (You can call the White House, no problem, and your number comes up. If you're not threatening, it's no problem.) I called and said, "Hi, I'm Nikki Giovanni. I'm a poet and I teach and wanted to know if I could go to the Panama Canal with the President.

And they said, "Miss Giovanni (actually they called me Dr. Giovanni) I don't think the President is going." "Well, the President must be going. Can you give me somebody who knows a little more than you?"

I'm just, it's an operator or something, you know. "Can I have the secretary to the secretary?" And so you get somebody else. I say, "Hi, it's Nikki Giovanni." They said, "We know that." By then they knew, and I said, "I just want to go to the Panama Canal with the President."

'Cause you can go if you're not a risk or something, you know. I mean, I'm doing something special. I mean anybody can do it; if you haven't been arrested and you aren't threatening these people, you can do it. You just have to pay for it.

And she said, "Dr. Giovanni, I don't think the President is going, but let me call you back." And I said, "I'd appreciate that because I'm sure the President is going because we have to give the canal back. And in giving it back, we need to give it back to the Panamanians. But we also need to stop by, and I wanted to mention that to Bill. We need to do something for Jamaica, so as we go down, we stop and give a nod, because they don't always know these things. If you don't tell them, how they gonna know?" Only made sense.

I did get a call back and she said, "Dr. Giovanni, I'm sorry, but the President is not going." I said, "That's okay; let me have Al Gore, because I was born in Tennessee. I was born in Knoxville. Let me have Gore; I'll go with Gore, you know, that's okay." I wasn't happy to go with Gore because I'm not a Gore fan like that but, what the hell? Vice President, so you go.

I got his secretary, who said, "I'm sorry, Mr. Gore isn't going either." I said, "I gotta tell ya, I'm not going any place with Madeline Albright. I'm just not going to do it." And I, well, you got your pride, and so if they are going to be tacky, I'm just not going to do it.

And so that's why I ended up going on this cruise. In deciding to go, I just thought you should know this about this point. In deciding to go on this cruise - see I do a thing because - I find out about this thing a long time ago, well, not a *long* time ago, about two years ago.

I don't do email and now I no longer answer my phone. My mother says I'm unfriendly and I don't mean to be unfriendly, it's just that most people that call you, you don't want to talk to them. If you want to talk to them, you would have called them. So you have to kind of leave a message. I used to say that, "You know I'm not here; please don't leave a message," but my mother said that was too unfriendly. Now I say, "Please leave a message."

And I don't answer the phone because you end up getting the Virginia State Police, and it's always eight o'clock in the morning, and it's always, "Will you contribute to the wounded patrolman?" And it's not that you don't want to contribute to the wounded patrolman, it's just that it's eight o'clock in the morning. And actually you don't, but they are the patrolman, they know where you live, they know your car, and so you always say, "Oh yes, please, let me contribute."

And so I realize that what you do is, you don't answer your phone, then you don't have to contribute to any of that crap. But I was in my den; I don't even have a phone in my bedroom anymore. I'm a 60s person; you only get bad news. People call you after midnight, you only get bad news.

So I'm in my den which has a phone, and the phone rings, and, I don't know if you listen to something, I always try to listen to something. I'm a big fan of something, so when something says something to me, I try to pay attention. And the phone rang, and something said, answer the phone. So I say, ah, I'll take a chance.

And I answered the phone and it was Rosemary. "Hey, Nikki, it's Rosemary." "Hey, Rosemary." Rosemary is the poetry editor from *Essence* magazine. I said, "Hey, Rosemary, how you doing?" "Well, we're fine. I just know that you can't guess what we were doing." I said, "No, Rosemary, actually I can't. You're totally right."

She said, "We were just having an editorial meeting." I said, "All righty and I really appreciate you letting me know. I'm packing because I am going away now."

She said, "No, no, no, Nikki, we realized we didn't have a poem for the 30th anniversary." I said, "Rosemary, what are you saying?" She said, "Would you like to write a poem?" I said, "Oh, gosh, yes, I was in the first edition of *Essence*." I said, "I would be thrilled to write a poem. I know the anniversary is May, so when would you like a poem, like February or early March?"

She said, "Nik, we were thinking Friday." I said, "Rosemary, it's Monday. I can't possibly do a poem that anybody would like between now and then." She told me who she would have to call if I said no, and I thought, oh God, not one more tacky poem, please, Lord. You get tired of those tacky poems.

So I said, "Give me a minute and I'll see what I can do. What did you guys have in mind because sometimes it helps to have a general theme." "Well, we're thinking about doing something for all the women who died in the 20th century." "Are you kidding? All of the women who died?"

She said, "I can fax it down to you." I said, "Rosemary, I know who died. I'm aware. I'm not stupid, you know, I don't need you to fax it down, but you can't write a poem for all the women who died." She said, "Well, if you can't do it, I'll just have to pass." I said, "I'll do it, I'll do it."

I gotta tell you, I'm a big fan of Daisy Bates. I've always loved Ms. Bates. Actually, I carry a bookmark with Daisy. I love a lot of people. This poem I'm gonna share, that I wanna share, is about those women. But Daisy Bates, but Daisy in red, I always thought was cool.

Now Mrs. Parks, as we all know, is a saint. Rosa will not appear in here, you know everybody, I mean, how can you not love Mrs. Parks? But Daisy Bates would do a thing, some of you remember Ms. Bates, and she would loop her thumbs in her belt and I always thought it was so cool. So when I was growing up I used to stand and practice my Daisy Bates attitude.

So I want to do a poem for people that I love like Daisy Bates, but then I realized I can't do a poem for everybody, so I needed to find somebody. And of course I thought about my grandmother 'cause I'm very close to my grandmother, and I do know that God couldn't be everyplace, and I know that is exactly what he did, he invented grandmothers. Because where would we be without our grandmothers?

It's the reason we hate Little Red Riding Hood. It's not that she was disobedient and stupid and a junkie; she was a junkie, she was in a poppy field, what was she doing there? She couldn't tell a wolf from a regular person; she's high as a kite. That's the truth and by the time she gets to grandmother, she can't tell her grandma, "What big eyes!' The girl had a drug problem, no question about it. It's the truth, but we hate her because she killed her grandmother.

But I thought about my grandmother, and I thought about all of those women who actually brought us through the 30s, 40s, and 50s. I don't know if you remember, I'm a southerner, I'm from Tennessee, and you remember they used to always, whenever they got ready to go out, they always went out dressed. Like we would go out, my generation, people my age, (I'm 57 now), when we got ready to demonstrate we'd put on jeans, we'd put on boots.

But when they got ready to go out, they always got dressed, and so they would take their baths, and they would have their Sweetheart Soap, and it seems like the world always smells like Sweetheart Soap. They'd take their bath with their Sweetheart Soap, and they would come out, and they were always hot because it was summer, so they had the body powder. And they would always make up their faces, they never left the house without making up their faces; it's a totally different world.

I don't even wear makeup, but they always did, so they would sit down at their dressing table and those were the days, for those of you who are too young to remember, when face powder came in a box.

And those were the days before they had pantyhose, because stockings had seams; you all who are younger don't remember that stockings had seams. And they always straightened their seams and that was way before they had things like garter belts, garter belts didn't come in till the late 60s, so they always had to roll it up with the garters. And for those of us who couldn't afford garters, what they would do is roll the stocking and then turn it and then tie it.

And they always, it was so wonderful to watch them get themselves together and they would go and they had that click, clack, click 'cause they walked with that determination, and when we start to think about who got us over, Clara Ward said, "How I got over my soul looks back." We never have to wonder because it was those women, and that's not to the exclusion of those men, but those women did everything that they could, and then they would turn around and say something sweet and wonderful.

I know my grandmother worked in service for a while, and they would come home at night after having been... of course, we didn't have any idea of the amount of work. They'd been on their feet all day cleaning somebody else's house, making somebody else's bed, doing somebody else's laundry, hanging it out, cooking, and then they had to steal what they had made and they would come home with a little piece of cake or a little piece of pie, piece of chicken, whatever it was that they had. It was so sweet, and they would shake you, and they'd wake you up, nine o'clock or ten o'clock at night, and they would say, "I got something for you."

And it would be so wonderful because this is what we now know to be the fruits of their labor, but they wanted you to know how important it was to them. And they would say, "Now, you go on back to sleep." And they would kiss you good night and it has never been so wonderful; those women will not be replicated. Whatever stars brought those women together, it can't be done again. We can only remember them. It's a hole, it's a hole in our hearts, because they were an extraordinary group.

And I wanted to write a poem for *Essence* for them, which is what I sat down to do, and I called it "What We Miss - A Eulogy." *Essence* published it last year as, "What We Miss - A Tribute." But it is a eulogy because they are gone. I'm next in line, I'm the next generation, I'm 57. And we are not them. We try, but we don't look like it, we don't have the style, we don't have the patience.

And, God forbid, whenever we lose Lena Horne, that's the last of the Harem Renaissance, is Lena. I am really cheering for both of them. I want Lena and Rosa Parks to live forever. I just do. I would love to see them get to be 150, 200 years old; oh, my, my, Lena still a grand old dame. I wrote a poem,

"What We Miss."
What we miss, the smell of Evening in Paris, or, sometimes,
Channel No. 5;
The bits of face powder left on the dressing table;
The little tubes of tasteful, not quite trashy, but still very hip,
red lipstick;
The almost empty bottles of off-pink fingernail polish.
We miss the old fan oscillating and the grunt of the girdle
resisting its chore;
The smell of Dixie peach waiting while the iron heats to do its
touch up.
We miss the instructions, I have to go to the church meeting
and you have to heat up the dinner I left it on the stove
and don't stand in front of the windows
and don't hang on the telephone if you don't know the voice
right away
and I'll be back as soon as I can, and absolutely we will miss
the click of the heels on the sidewalk as they hurried off
proud angry determined urging us on.
What we miss the excited chatter spreading the good news of
victory
or the horrible news of setbacks. Always wondering why
questioning when, hoping now or at least soon,

we miss the gathering of the book club or the garden club,
the Delta Alpha Zeta Sorority Missionary Society,
the quilting bee, the Wednesday night prayer group,
the voices lifted in prayer or song or irritation calling for a
better tomorrow,
whatever better may be, but knowing whatever better is;
is change from that which cannot be tolerated today
so tomorrow must be sought defined embraced and prepared
for.
And those voices from those women urged us on.
What we understood that women had to work at home and at
jobs
then give back for reading hour at the library or girl scouts or
Try-Hi-Y
then raise money for city kids to go to camp in the country
and country kids to see Washington DC, our nation's capital
and all the other things women had to do to stay sane
and as women they did, largely without complaint always
without remorse
frequently without encouragement but always urging us on
because he may not come when you call but always comes on
time.
And we have to be ready for any number of calls to lead
hundreds of slaves to freedom, to report a lynching, to pilot an
airplane,
to guide nine children through a murderous mob,
to sculpt, to write novels and plays and poems,
to dance all over Paris and defeat the Nazis with the courage of
the rainbow tribe,
to sing arias and those soul-cleansing blues
to do anything we are called to do because nobody is better
than you
and we believe that because of the conviction in those voices
urging us on.
But we accept the love the challenge the hope they offered
the necessity to remember, the vision to follow in their
footsteps while blazing new trails.

What we miss, the sight of those black women walking down
sidewalk-less streets carrying brown bags full of groceries or
leftovers,
or winter clothes in summer and summer clothes in winter
chiding us for missing church, applauding us for school work
or the recital, acknowledging some small deed we did, finding
something good and uplifting to say urging us on.

[*Applause*]

Thank you. I really like that. This is a poem and I'm not going
to story-tell you to death. Just a couple of things 'cause there is no
point in being live if you are going to do that.

Most of you are black in this room, and maybe some of you
who are not, but most of you who are black, know that this is the
kitchen. It is, and I don't know why it's called that. But it is and
people, like, when you were a little girl, people would just say to
you, strangers practically, "Come here, baby, let me touch up
your kitchen" right?"

And people are always trying to get your hair straightened
out and, I think I mentioned, I don't know why they do that, but
black women are sick when it comes to hair. They are always
doing something. When I was a little girl I lived with
Grandmother, and something we did every summer, you go
down to your grandmother's, and I always enjoyed it because it
always sort of made sense.

For those of us who were Northern kids going South, you
know, they kept you busy. So if you went to visit Grandmother,
from Monday to Friday you had vacation Bible school, on Sunday,
of course, you had church, and then you had the program after
church, and then you had Sunday night prayer meeting, so you
stayed in church all day. So the only time you could sleep late
would have been Saturday.

But my grandmother had a rule which, for some reason my
grandfather went for it, and that's that she never cleaned up. She
would cook but he had to clean up, which would have worked,

and it didn't bother me that much, except that on Saturday, because Grandmother was a pretty woman, I think that Grandpapa was always worried that somebody would say something to Grandmother.

And Grandmother's one of those people who didn't take it lightly, and so he knew if he let Grandmother go to the market, (and for those of you who know Knoxville, Gay Street had the market), Gay Street was the main street in Knoxville. If Grandpapa had let Grandmother go to the market, what would have happened is that somebody would have said something to her like, "Levinia, you looking good today."

She would have come back and said, "John Brown the butcher said I was looking good." He would have then had to go uptown (he's from Georgia, you see, ugly things happened) he would have to take his gun, go up there, shoot the butcher. The crowd would have come, they would have to lynch Grandpapa, maybe burn the house down, ugly things happen.

And Grandpapa was a very thoughtful man so Grandpapa did the shopping, which meant on Saturday morning I had to do the cleaning which was okay but Grandmother was one of those people who could do vicious things happily. So at 6 o'clock in the morning, which was when she got up to start the coffee, she would come into your room, and then she would shake you, it's time to get up, which she knew damn well you didn't want to get up at this hour.

She wanted to fix breakfast and so she had things for you to do, and so we all ate breakfast together, and then Grandpapa got dressed and went to town 'cause he was a gentleman, always wore a tie, always wore his suspenders, right? Flapped his sleeves and went uptown to do the shopping.

That left me to clean up after Grandmother, which was okay. And then she would say something like, "Let's dust the house." Only it wasn't a "let's"; I dusted the house and she came behind me. You don't actually know me, but I gotta tell you, you can take my word for it, I love dusting. It's the next thing to being a poet because whatever it is you are doing you are finished with it. And I would take, and this was before you had Pledge and things you could spray, these were in days when you have the Johnsons wax in a can and you had the rag, and you could easily streak if you weren't good, but I'm good. And I would do the table, and I would do it all, and I would be finished, like, 10 o'clock, and Grandmother's one of those people would come behind you, it was one of her unattractive habits, and she would come behind, "Oh, you finished."

I used to wax the floor in the pantry because I wanted the mice, (we live in the country), I thought if we had the wax smell the mice would realize somebody was watching and they wouldn't come in and wouldn't get in the trap. You didn't want to kill them and you didn't want them around, you just wanted to – sniff - "Oh yeah, somebody lives here," and go on. And so I would be finished by 10 o'clock.

We all have ambitions when we are growing up. You have talents, you have skills, and what I always thought I could do, and I did because I am very good at it, I always thought I would be an Olympic swinger. I always thought that swinging, it should be, if they can have synchronized swimming as an Olympic event, they definitely should have double dutch, right? Sure, and I always thought they should have swinging, and I grew up with real swings.

Some of you all don't know real swings, you know the swings from recycle. I grew up with iron bars in cement in the ground, and you had the chains that were down, and it was real low, so here's the deal for those of you who don't know swinging. What you want to do is stand in the swing and pump it up, and you pump it up, and pump it up, and what you want to do was go even with the bars.

Now Physics 101 tells us when you do that, there is this moment that time sort of stops, and then it drops. So this is where the skill comes. When you go even with the bars, it's going to drop, and you have to hold on, look cool as it drops, and then drop back into the bottom. And you swing a couple of more times, and then you dismount. And that's what you actually practiced, so it's like a poor girl's parallel bars. It's what you do, so you just working on your skills.

So I would go across the street to the park and I would work on the skills and eventually Grandmother would call me, saying, "Nikki, come on in, it's time for lunch." And I always liked Grandmother for this. I complained about this, but I liked her for this. She always treated you like you had sense, so you were expected to read the paper.

So we would have lunch, it was the only time that we had lunch together 'cause Grandpapa was gone. And she would say, "What about yak, yak, yak," and you were supposed to answer, which I did. And after lunch I would clean up and then, this is the sad part, then she would say to me, "Now go on up to Letha's and get your hair done."

Letha, to me, is Mrs. Allen, Letha Allen, and she ran the barber shop. Now I know that all of us in this room aren't black, so those of us who aren't may not know what it is like to go into a black beauty parlor. Okay, 'cause it's a whole trip the rest of you all know. So when you go to the beauty parlor and got all of these black women, and they are all lined up facing the door, everybody wanted to know what was going on.

So you would open the door and, I'm not shy but I am cautious, so I would open the door and just kind of hang there till somebody noticed you. And somebody would invariably say, "Who's that?" And somebody else would say, "That's Lou Watson's grandbaby." And somebody would say, "Which daughter?" 'cause Grandmother had three daughters. And somebody would say, "I think that's the oldest girl, I think that's Yolan's girl."

I'm standing there, I don't know what I look like, but I have basic intelligence. I know who my grandmother is, I know who my mother is, I know my name. But, of course, it never occurred to them to ask me, and I knew something that, for those of you who don't know, I knew not to answer. Until they asked me. I knew that.

So somebody would say, "Come on in, baby," and I would say, "Thank you," because I was always polite. Close the door and come in and then you hear the words you do not want to hear. And they'd say, "Have a seat." Now, I grew up in a world that children did not have appointments or times. Children went, and as long as there was no adult to be taken care of, they could be waited on, but if an adult came in, you got put aside. So you just got set up to tell the truth.

I didn't know then that I was going to be a writer, but I never minded, you know, some kids fidget, I don't fidget. And I would just sit down and I would listen, and eventually they would notice that you were listening, and that would disturb them. You'd hear so-and-so is going with so-and-so's husband, you just kinda wanna get a visual on who said it, so you can go back and ask Grandma and say, "Well, Miss Smith said so-and-so."

You just wanted to keep up, and they did that, "Little pitchers have big ears" and things like that, but eventually someone would say, "Come, I'm going to wash you out now." Miss Allen had two sinks, so that was good. So you got washed out and, of course, they wrapped your head in a towel. And what you were hoping was that the dryer, 'cause she only had one dryer that came over your head, was empty and you could get your head dried. If not, you would sit there for however long it took.

Eventually somebody would say, "Come on." Usually there was some apprentice there and that's what always bothered you, 'cause it was Saturday and there's a lot of people in there. The little apprentice would say, "I'll press you out." It's like "Oh no!" 'cause you know what happened. I grew up knowing the most normal thing in the world was a little burn. Everybody had a burn 'cause you got your hair done. And then Miss Allen would come and give you your curls, and you had your curls, and I'm gonna tell you this 'cause maybe you don't know, maybe some of you don't know this, the reason women my age don't swim, and they don't, they don't, is because of what I just described.

So by the time you get home, it's 4 or 5 o'clock in the afternoon. It's still summer, its hot, so Grandmother would say - this is during the age of segregation so the swimming pool in Knoxville was in Mechanicsville – "You wanna go over to Mechanicsville and go swimming,?" and I said, "Yes, I want to go," and I did want to go, and I would go, but I wouldn't think of getting in the water because of all that I had just been through.

And women my age don't swim because, say what you wanna say about the swimming cap, the swimming cap will keep *that* dry but right around *here* the water would come in. There is a process in black circles known as "go back." Your hair would go back, you wouldn't think about it, thank God for the natural, but you enjoyed.

Eventually we got old enough to date, and so you're trying to date, but where do you date in Knoxville, Tennessee? So the grandmothers and the resident parents all got together and had dances for us at the Phyllis Wheatly Y, which was lovely.

So after supper, you all do know supper 'cause you have dinner, so after supper, Grandmother would wanna walk me up. And, of course, I didn't wanna walk up with Grandmother, I wanted to walk up with a boy, but you couldn't really walk up with a boy. But maybe on good days when she wasn't feeling much like walking up with me, she would let me walk with another girlfriend, you know, so you didn't look like your grandmother was dropping you off.

And we would dance, and I'm still amazed that black women have any kind of social life for the same reason. And you would go and you would dance, and it's all right, you're doing a fast dance, but, being Southern women, we all carried handkerchiefs. You had your little white handkerchief, we all had our little one, and you'd pat yourself when you were sweating.

But the boys didn't carry handkerchiefs, and so, when the slow songs came on, the boys would come over, 'cause they never really said, "Will you dance?" and all of us were like, "No, I don't want to dance." It's amazing, and it wasn't that we didn't want to dance, it's that, if we had danced, he would have put his head next to my head and then this part of your hair would go back. That's the truth. And you'd go home and your grandmother would know that you had been grinding at the Y. That was a no no, that was a huge no no.

I wrote this poem because everybody takes care of this kitchen and basically this is not the kitchen that's nappy. The kitchen that is nappy is your life, so I just wanted to recommend, this is a poem about wife abuse, so I want to recommend against you hitting your wife. Not only do I think it's a bad idea, but that's between you and your wife, and I'm not trying to get in between you and your wife. Whatever you and your wife do is up to you.

Let me just say this about your daughter. If you beat your wife on Saturday or Friday night, you come in, you're drunk, she's home, you start beating on her, your daughter sees that, a couple of things happen. One, it scares her and, two, she starts to say to herself, "Well, Daddy's a good man, everybody says Daddy's a good man. He works, he brings the money home, if it wouldn't be for him drinking on Friday night, coming in, beating on Momma, everything would be fine."

So your daughter starts to think, "Well, maybe good men come in on the weekend and beat their wives. So if my boyfriend is beating me, maybe that's what should happen." So now you see your daughter, and she got a black eye, she got a tooth hanging out, she got bruises all up and down her arm, you wanna go kill somebody. You need to ask yourself, "Where did she learn to take that?" She learned that by watching what you did to her mother.

Let me say this about your son, your son's just a little boy, he's just home, he watches his father come in on Saturday night drunk beating up on his mother, and he says, "Daddy's a good man 'cause everybody says that daddy's a good man, maybe what good men do to women that they love is beat on them, so maybe what I should learn to beat on a woman that I love." So you're watching now your daughter-in-law carrying your grandchildren, your son's kicking her in the stomach and going crazy and you're trying to tell him, "Don't do that." But he can't hear you because he saw you for the last ten or fifteen years beating on his mother.

So I am going to suggest that you maybe take a walk around the park, maybe join the Police Athletic League and hit yourself a medicine ball. But don't be beating on some woman the only reason you can beat on her is that she is home loving you. So whatever else is wrong with you, get a life and stop that craziness.

I wrote this poem because one day you gonna have a stroke, and you're not going to be able to walk anyplace. And you're gonna be sitting there trying to tell your daughter, "You know I didn't mean it, baby," but you damn well did, and your daughter is gonna sit there and look at you and say, "I think you're going to hell, Daddy." Why do that when you know you're gonna be sorry.

I wrote a poem and it's a sad poem called "The Wrong Kitchen," 'cause everybody takes care of this one but nobody takes care of the one you living in.

Grandmother would sit me
between her legs
 to scratch my dandruff
and unravel my plaits

we didn't know then
that dandruff was a sign of nervousness
hives tough emotional decisions
things seen that were better
unseen.

We thought love could cure
anything a doll here a favorite
caramel cake there

the arguments, the slaps, the chairs
banging against the wall,

the plea's to please stop
that disappear under quilts aired
in fresh air,
would be forgotten after Sunday school
teas and presentations to the book club.

I didn't know then why I played
my radio all night
and why I kept a light burning.
We thought back then that it was my hair
that was nappy

so we trying to make it alright
straightened the wrong kitchen.

Honest to God, last story. Well, it's the Zora Neale Hurston Festival. Speaking of the President, I did get invited to the White House once. And I don't think I'll be invited back anytime soon. No, I was thrilled.

I live in a little town and well, actually, Orlando's a city but Eatonville is a little town. And Maitland's a little town. There are a lot of little towns around here and everybody knows your business where I live and people are friendly.

But Charlie is my mailman, and one day, I have a dog, I need to tell you her name is Wendy, and Wendy's overweight and really sweet and she's a Cairn Terrier. very territorial. And one day Wendy was barking, and occasionally, 'cause we get packages and things, you owe your mail carrier money. It's not like a big city where they'll take it back. You know they just give it to you and say you owe me a nickel, you owe me a dime.

Wendy was barking, barking, barking, and I thought, oh my God. I looked out and it was Charlie, and I thought I must owe him a fortune because they never wait. So I grabbed my piggy bank and went out and said, "Hey Charlie, I'm sorry, I must owe you a dollar or a dollar-and-a-half by now."

He said, "No, no, Nikki, you don't owe me anything." "Oh," I said, "the dog was barking, I must owe you something." "No, no, you don't, uh, you don't owe me anything." I said, "Oh, how you doing?" He said, "I'm fine, how you doing?" I said, "Fine, fine, everything's fine." "Well, I'm just delivering the mail," and I said, "Well, Charlie, it's what you do."

He said, "Yeah, I just happened to notice this envelope here, I just happened to notice it." I said, "What is it, Charlie?" "Well, it's the White House, it looks like it's from the White House. I think it's an invitation." I said, "Well, Charlie, if you wanna give it to me, I'll open it, and we'll see." He said, "Okay, sure, yeah." So he gave it to me.

I said, "Charlie, it's an invitation to the White House." He said, "A dinner or what?" I said, "Yes, it's a dinner invitation." He said, "Okay, I thought it was a dinner invitation." "Well, yeah, it sure is." "Well," he said, "you going?" I said, "Yeah, Charlie, actually I think I'll go."

He said, "Okay, well, I gotta go. I can't just hang around all day." "Okay, so, you know, Charlie, just say 'Nikki got an invitation to the White House, she's going'." So I say that's really cool.

Now the White House doesn't give you lead time. And I've been talking about Black people, but I think it's probably fair to say black women always have one new thing in the closet, 'cause you never know when somebody gonna die, when somebody gonna get married, you know. I'm not saying white women don't, but I know black women always have one new thing. And I had a new suit but I didn't have anything to go with it, and the White House doesn't give you what you call lead time. So I said to myself, "Oh my God," like all the other little old ladies, I said, "I need to get to New York. I need to buy something to wear with the suit."

And so, of course, by this time I'm going down and my airport is at Roanoke, and I get to Roanoke, I get to USAir, and I'm saying, "Hey, how you doing? I need to go to New York." And he said, "Yeah, you going to the White House, you gotta go get something to wear." I said, "Yeah." They said, "We thought you might be down, Ms. Giovanni."

They are very nice, they always call me "Ms. Giovanni." "We thought you might be down, Ms. Giovanni, so we going to give you the seven-day fare 'cause we know you didn't have any lead time." I said, "I really appreciate that," and I did what anybody else would do, pulled out my MasterCard, and I handed it to him, and they swiped it.

And you know it's not right, I mean nobody is going to give somebody a MasterCard, you know what I'm saying, that it's $200.00 in arrears. You know, I think that they should have to say what's pushing it over, so, usually, it's like $10.30, which case you can pay it, you know. So you get the $200.00 ticket, you pay $190.00 on the MasterCard.

And so it was embarrassing, it came up, you know, declined, and they said, "Ms. Giovanni, it declined, but it must be a mistake. We know you work at Tech." And I said, "I work at Tech, I do, yeah, I do." "It must be a mistake, we'll just run it later on. It must be something in the wire, must be something in the wire."

And I don't want you to think I don't pay my bills because I do. I pay my bills, but it's just one of those things, you pay the bills off every month. You pay bills, but people don't just want you to pay bills, people don't want you to just pay the bill, they want you to pay the bill on a certain day. And so you're a half an hour late, and, all of a sudden, the card is bitching and moaning and declining and carrying on like you not going to pay them eventually. It just makes you crazy, you know? I was really glad, it was very sweet of them.

So I got on the plane, and I go on and get to New York because that's where all the old ladies go, caught a cab and went to Saks Fifth Avenue 'cause I have a Saks charge. 'Cause everybody, everybody, you have to have a Saks charge 'cause that is how you know you're grown. And I'll be paying Saks when I'm dead, the estate will be paying Saks. But, you know, Saks is where

Aretha Franklin owed them $200,000.00, and they were upset about it, but somebody approved Aretha at $175,000.00. They need to blame themselves on that. They don't let me run my account like that.

So, I went to Saks. I found this really beautiful blouse. I pull out my Saks charge, everybody's happy, she goes to run the charge and, I hope none of you have ever heard that 'cause it's a bad sound, your sales clerk comes back, (because they are always so discreet), "Ms. Giovanni, they want to talk to you."

But you don't want to talk to them because whatever they have to say is not going to make you happy, and so you pick up the phone, and you say, "Oh no, not them, I need the blouse. I was invited to the White House and you gotta approve this charge. I can't understand, I'll pay you people." Then, "Ms. Giovanni, I'm going to approve the charge, but tell me this? Don't you want to pay something this month?" Honestly, I loved her for that question, of course, I wanted to. What would make her think I didn't want to? It wasn't a want, it was a need, it was a can. So I could honestly say, "Yes, I do want to pay you something this month."

I gotta tell you, I went on to the White House and it was really a lot of fun and I enjoyed it but I ended up writing this poem. I was talking about space. This is a poem called "Sound and Space." It's a love poem, and I ended up writing this poem 'cause everybody always on to space and what is going on.

They always talk about the black holes, and there is no such thing as a black hole. It's not black and it's not a hole. It's just prejudice that makes people say that. It's the truth, you think about space. You see, what it is, is an energy that, once it's encountered, people find a peace and a beauty.

And I think of black people like that. And so people try and put bad terms on us so that people don't want to come and be close to us, and experience the peace and the beauty. So I wrote a poem called "Sound and Space."

It's as if you have been invited to the White House, and you know you're gonna smile, so you want your teeth to be right, white, bright, and you brush and brush, but because you have a partial plate you are mostly brushing your gums. And, quite naturally, since you want to look fabulous and make the First Lady green with envy because you have on your only designer suit and a blouse that, if you were quite honest, you couldn't actually afford.

But the girl in Saks was so nice, and the girl that approved the charge heard the panic in your voice, and she, after all, had never been invited to the White House and, what's more probably, never would be. So she said, "Why yes, I will approve this charge, but do you think you might want to pay us something this month?" And you said, "Absolutely," because you do want to pay something. It's just that Saks runs up against Nordstrom's and Neiman Marcus, not to mention food and shelter. So, yes, absolutely, you want to, but maybe you will, and maybe you can't.

And that's what so hard for people to understand - that distance between want and able, and that's what we need to talk about. So, of course, I remember Lena Horne singing about polka-dots and moonbeams, and my grandmother being totally delighted with the RCA Victor TV, and her saying to Grandpapa, "We better get Nikki up because Lena Horne is on TV." And me not quite knowing who Lena Horne was at that point, though now recognizing that she was a great lady who has fought long and hard for civil rights, who is also a lady of Delta Sigma Theta, and who looks so fabulous in Gap jeans, and all the world now wants to be 80 years old and look that good. So the Gap was very smart to ask to photograph Lena in those jeans.

But that's not the point of her being on TV when very few black people were on television, whether or not they were very talented. And haven't we come a long way though, quite naturally, we have a way to go. But my grandmother always said, "If you make a dollar, save a dime."

It's not that my grandfather in anyway disagreed, but he was more casual about the needing and having, so, I am sure it was Grandmother that saved for the RCA Victor TV, and even at that I have to acknowledge that she was so intrigued with Nipper that even if it had done nothing more than show the dog responding to his master's voice, Grandmother would have thought she made a good purchase, though the TV also brought us Lena Horne.

So Grandmother was a believer and so am I and that, too, is a bit off-point if only because it was Billie Holiday who sang the definitive *I Wished on the Moon* for something I never knew, and to hear her sing like that, even though because dumb restrictive drug rules that punish some people for some drugs though not others. She would never be on television which was a total loss to those of us who wished on the moon while observing strange fruits that travel light, and we knew hearing that Holiday moan that the moon granted wishes. So I started singing, thinking that if I could throw a note high enough and strong enough there would be the possibility that it would be heard somewhere in space, and that is what I want to talk about here.

Science teaches us there is no sound in space, and I think that is hogwash, because if there were no sound in space how would all those wishes get up to the moon? And anyone with an ounce of sense knows science fiction is much better than science fact, because science fact tries to prove that Thomas Jefferson wasn't diddling Sally Hemings, and everybody knows people diddle people all the time especially when they can't say no!

So yes, there is sound in space, and a large part of it says, "I love you" in a lot of different ways. And when the language is unknown to the hearer, other people say things like, "that's gibberish," but love can never be gibberish, foolish for sure, silly you bet, but the basis of all relationships is love, which is then followed by trust and not the other way around, because if trust was the basis, there would be world peace and safe international travel.

But what I want to point out, since it is always important to do something useful, is that you should quite naturally floss. And well, you should. I don't want you to waste your time with me without learning anything, and nickels and dimes have a relationship with dollars and cents, but not halves and quarters. And machines will tell you, deposit more money, good luck when it isn't luck that you need, it's good science. Which would explain why and how, why, when all is said and done, we are left with this density that forces us to recognize the ego-nebula is fallen into itself and will one day be a planet but mostly we will not be around to see it.

And then there are those troublesome black holes which are so totally fascinating but no one can put their finger on what makes them so important. And I'm here to tell you, I know the density of a black hole does not prevent light from escaping, but rather one's light encounters the black hole. It finds such beauty and peace and comfort it no longer needs to search, which is another word for love, and I do. Thank you.

Ego Tripping (there may be a reason why)

I was born in the Congo
I walked to the fertile crescent and built
    the sphinx
I designed a pyramid so tough that a star
    that only glows every one hundred years falls
    into the center giving divine perfect light
I am bad

I sat on the throne
    drinking nectar with Allah
I got hot and sent an ice age to Europe
    to cool my thirst
My oldest daughter is Nefertiti
    the tears from my birth pains
    created the Nile
I am a beautiful woman

I gazed on the forest and burned
    out the Sahara Desert
    with a packet of goat's meat
    and a change of clothes
I crossed it in two hours
I am a gazelle so swift
    so swift you can't catch me

    For a birthday present when he was three
I gave my son Hannibal an elephant
    He gave me Rome for Mother's Day
My strength flows ever on
My son Noah built new/ark and
I stood proudly at the helm
    as we sailed on a soft summer day
    I turned myself into myself and was
Jesus
    men intone my loving name
    All praises All praises
I am the one who would save

I sowed diamonds in my back yard
My bowels deliver uranium
    the filings from my fingernails are
    semi-precious jewels
    On a trip north
I caught a cold and blew
My nose giving oil to the Arab world
I am so hip even my errors are correct
I sailed west to reach east and had to round off
    the earth as I went
    The hair from my head thinned and gold was laid
    across three continents
I am so perfect so divine so ethereal so surreal
I cannot be comprehended except by my permission

I mean...I...can fly
    like a bird in the sky...

N.Y. Nathiri:

Ms. Giovanni has agreed to some Q&A for those of you who would like to stay and ask a few questions or make comments. We do have a reception in the cafeteria and she will be signing books for those of you who would like. So please take a few minutes more and stay with us and expand your opportunity to be with her.

Nikki Giovanni:

I can tell you I am heartbroken. Let me start with that. Well, Serena Williams lost to Martina Hingis, and Serena and Venus were upset by Kournikova. And so now it's up to Venus to beat Martina, please, and then of course little fat ass Lindsay [Davenport]. Excuse me, children, I just thought I would share that for those of you who hadn't stayed caught up. I was just heartbroken.

It's because my plane was late. I said to my mother when I was getting ready to come, I said to her, "I'm gonna get to Florida to pull her through," and something happened to that stupid plane in Charlotte and we sat on the ground. By the time we actually took off and I could concentrate on Serena, she had lost. So I'm maybe thinking about suing USAir.

Yes, Mama, somebody had their hand up.

Female Attendee:

First of all I just wanted to say that I am so glad to be here this evening, I'm so glad you are with us. I am thirty years old. My dad brought me here. I have been a fan since I was 12 years old ....

Nikki Giovanni:

Thank you, and thank you for the good wishes.

Yes ma'am.

Male Attendee:

I was curious. You were very active in the 60s. Do you see a new surge in the 90s?

Nikki Giovanni:

I'm familiar with American labor. I'm ashamed of myself I haven't really read a paper since what's his name got, and I need to be, I'm aware of Seattle. American labor is in trouble because labor wanted to ignore the legitimate needs of its black and brown brothers in the United States.

And now that American business, I think Converse is the last tennis people, and they have just moved into Asia. Now that American business has shown that they would rather be rich than... White labor is beginning to realize that they have something in common with the rest of the working people.

And so when we look at, and there is a God if you ever thought there wasn't, Linda Chavez had to withdraw from the Labor Secretary. Was that the most cynical thing that you ever in your life? I had the occasion of debating Ms. Chavez once, and the only reason I accepted the debate is that it was in Yellow Springs, Ohio, and I 'm from Ohio, so that I knew my family and friends would be there. That's the truth. I'm not a fool and everything they applauded, everything she said they booed. Which was as it should be, 'cause that was the only reason I went.

I got a call from the American Enterprise Institute and they said, "We would love for you to come to D.C., Linda said she enjoyed talking with you." I said, "Linda did not say that because Linda was made to be a fool, and I know that she didn't say that. But I have to earn a living too, so here's my price to come."

And they said, "Oh, we thought you would enjoy the publicity." And I said, "No, what I would enjoy is the check," because no, you got to admit sometimes that's what you do it for; other times you do it differently.

But I dislike Ms. Chavez and so I was out of the country when I saw that W. had put her up for Labor Secretary of all things. And I really did say, "Get that bitch," because I know that anybody that thinks like she does, anybody can tell anybody that the minimum wage is a sufficient wage is evil, because it's not. It's not. And labor, we need to go up because the people that are saying you and I can live off of the minimum wage are making not hundreds of thousands but hundreds of millions!

And it's so vicious and crazy. So what I've seen of the new activism is that labor finally realizes they are in trouble and so they need to make a pact, not for United States but around. Labor has to do better because it's not just a question of, "Look we are in a ..."

This is a teeny tiny planet; I'm just a poet and I know that. It's time we made compact with the people who do work. We all do work. Even rich people work. I'm not trying to kill rich people off. Jesus said its easier for a camel to go through a needle's eye than a rich man to go to heaven. I believe that, but some rich people don't care where they go they just want to be rich while they are here.

We need to tax these people because they're still going to be so much rich. What if we capped it? And it tickles me because poor people will have this argument, "Well, he ought to be able to make what he wants to make, okay?"

But what if we said, no family of four can accrue income over $100 million per annum? $100 million - that's still richer than all of us put together, most likely. They are still very rich, but then they say no, and poor people don't have a pot to piss in or a window to throw it out of. Sit around and say you ought to be able to get what you have, but you don't have anything because somebody else is sitting on the resources. So what I think about the activism? There has to be a new economic justice.

We can do only what we can do. That's a tautology, isn't it? If there is one thing that I like about myself, there's some things that I do and some that I don't, but one that I do is: I accept limitations. I'm very easy, I'm a good patient, I'm very good at...somebody said I was quixotic but I'm not quixotic. I know exactly what I'm doing and I know most of the battles I fight I'm going to lose. To be quixotic is to think that somehow you're going to win this thing. I don't think so, so you just do what you have to do whatever the consequences are.

And so to be a poet or to be a human being is to admit whatever it is, to deal with the truth. Bush is an evil man and so is his daddy. He is, and so you say that you know eventually people won't hire you, whatever is going to happen gonna' happen, but at least you can always look at yourself and you know, well, he's still...

There was a story I heard and I said I wasn't going to do any more stories. This is a Zora Neale Hurston kind of story. It's a black-and-white story and this is very nice story. And like eight-year-old kids on a playground, and the black kid and the white kid, two boys were fighting, and I really don't know who was supposed to be getting the best of whom at that point, but the white kid finally stepped back and said, "You're a nigger." And the black kid looked at him and said, "So?"

I love that. I thought, "YES, that has nothing to do with the fact that I whipping your butt." I love it so! I think that you just try to do what you can do when it comes up. It's an old expression in the black community, what you spend most of your life trying to do: you try not to laugh if it ain't funny, you try not to scratch if it don't itch.

And that will take a lot of your energy because, you would be surprised, people come in and say the weirdest things to you like you supposed to agree with them. And you just go, "What did I miss?" And it takes a lot of courage to do that. It takes a lot of courage to say, "Well, I didn't appreciate that." And people say, "Well, I didn't mean anything." Well, then, don't say it; you're too old to not mean anything; and you just have to keep fighting.

You fight wherever you are, you fight with the soldiers you have on the terrain that you find yourself, and write your poems and try to stay sane and try to be happy, because life's still about happiness and you just cannot let them take your...

That's one thing I like about black people, to be honest with you, and I think it's so fantastic. I'm teaching a course right now called "The Negro Spiritual, the American Metaphor." And I really didn't think anybody was going to sign up for it because who signs up for a course called "The Negro Spiritual," right? And there is seventy kids and its very balanced.

Virginia Tech is predominantly white but it's very balanced, but I would say I have about 40 white kids and about 35 blacks, so it's that way because it is the nature of Tech. And we sing, so we been singing spirituals. We sing "Steal Away", we made a hush harbor and we come together, and "Steal Away" was (they are looking it up right now) but you know that was the one that Nat Turner, they think Nat Turner wrote that.

So it's been really fun to bring these youngsters together and I'm saying to them all the time, because the white kids just looking at you, I don't dislike anybody, and I won't have anybody tell me that I do, because I don't. But I always say to the kids, "It's so nice to be black. I mean if you had a choice, it really is. I just so recommend this because it's true. Because we have this, this ability to go where the - and it's not that we don't knife each other and it's not that we don't do mean things, we do - but as a people we have this ability to bring this joy.

And it's like a cosmic responsibility. Who else in slave, in shadow slavery, could bring the sun out? And we can deal with the, "You got to walk this lonesome valley, you got to walk it by yourself. Sometimes I feel like a motherless child." We know the plaintiveness. But then you got the, "I've got a crown up in heaven. Ain't that good news?" What you gonna do about somebody in shadow slavery talking about, "Ain't that good news?"

On my journey now. Mt. Zion. Blacks found a way to be joyful. It such a wonderful thing to be black I do, I just, just, sometimes you wake up in awe, you just having your coffee. I am from a wonderful people, it just makes you happy. It really does.

Female attendee:
What words of wisdom can you give us parents …

Nikki Giovanni:

I think it's not the easiest story to tell, in many respects, and I think it's difficult to be a parent, I really do, no matter what color, race, religion. I think it's difficult because the one thing that you see, I'm not vast rich, I'm comfortable, but I think it's very hard because we all want our children to do better.

And in wanting our children to do better we don't want to put the burden. Like me, there are things that I hate and it's just because of the way I grew up. I hate amusement parks, I really couldn't begin to tell you. I grew up in Knoxville, Tennessee. Blacks were allowed to go to Chilhowie Park, you know, once on August the 8th and I found that to be unacceptable when I was a kid, so you can imagine. And I was born and actually grew up in Cincinnati where my parents were. And Coney Island did not admit blacks, so I grew up really hating and you have a child who's looking at Kings Island and it's a whole 'nother world out there.

Fortunately I had a good friend Connie, and Connie had three daughters and I just had one son, so she would take the kids to the amusement park because she liked to do it. And I never said to Thomas, I mean he was grown before I said, "I hate it." I do; it's so insulting that you have to beg somebody to let you have fun. That's what the spiritual is all about - they say we may not be able to, but we can find something else. But you want your kid to grow up saying, "I can ride the roller coaster, I can do the..." and so you let them go.

I don't go to movies, even now, even now I'm 57 and I know in my head, I know I can go and sit in a movie theatre where I want but I just resent asking those people to take money that I worked hard for. And most of the movies I don't care about. I must go to the movies, if I get lucky, every other year. I just hate it, I can't begin to tell you, but again, you don't want your child to grow up with your hatreds and I don't want my child to grow up hating anybody.

I wanted him to grow up feeling that the world I had an argument with... Thomas, one morning we lived in New York, speaking of South Bronx, and he went to school at Riverside. He went to kindergarten at Riverside and so we used to take the bus. We lived at 92nd and Central Park West. We used to take the bus up and one day he was late and I was fussing, you know how you fussing at him, and I don't know what it was, but I was fussing and I said, "What you gonna do when you find out everybody doesn't love you?"

It made the whole bus. You know how New York buses are; the whole bus went quiet. And Thomas said, "They don't?" Everybody on the bus went, "Aww." And I thought, "Well, I'm doing my job because, what I've done is, convinced this kid (that I'm about to kill for whatever reason it was) that not just Mommy but everybody loves you, and that's all you're trying to do. What does the song say? If anybody asks you who you are, tell them, "I'm a child of God," and that's all you're trying to do; you're saying the same thing to your children that our parents and grandparents said to us, "You as good as anybody else. You can be anything you want to be."

It sounds kind of superficial but you're doing that and, of course, we're ending up in debt with our children in a way that our parents... I went to Fisk University where tuition was $500.00 a semester. I don't have to tell that I didn't pay that to send him to Morehouse or Georgetown but we're just trying to help moving them along.

All I know is they're ours and all I know about whatever it is, is yours as long as it is yours. My mother say, "Let me know what you're doing; I'm going to stand between you and everybody else." That's not exactly what she said but that's what she meant. You know what she said and she was right. And that's what I think, and that's what we tell our children because anything else that's going to happen is normal.

It's not a good idea - I had a girlfriend whose daughter was expecting and she was very upset she's pregnant, and I said,

"Well, that's what happens, it does. It's not a good idea you got the grandchild but she still has to go to college so you have a job.

I had a son so it's not going to come to me the same way, it's true, but, mothers, actually sons are keeping the kids a lot more. But mothers of daughters have so many other problems because you are trying to say it's a mean world out there, and the daughters are saying everybody really loves me. And a lot of people might, but a lot more people are going to want to screw her before they are going to want to love her. And so all you're trying to do, you understand what I'm saying, is protect her.

And I did say to my son, "The reason God invented college was for sex because nothing else much happens in college." So isn't that why you and I studied, so we could go and have sex because you couldn't in high school because it wasn't allowed.

And so that's what we do, we say, "You cannot screw in high school. High school is for education you have to get, then you go away to college. Then you go away from Mommy and you don't call her, and then you do that, that's the way it works. And you take care of yourself, and you call me when you have a problem. But if you're smart, call me all the time, then I won't know when you are calling me with the problem and I'll answer my phone."

Because all you're trying to do is make sure that she's all right and what you want to do is get her through the next two years. I'm not picking on your daughter or anybody but you want to get them to be 18 or 19 years old and then what can you do? You can go to bridge club and say, "Hell I did my part, she's a fool." That's all you're trying to do.

So I don't have any advice; I just think we do our best, that's all. We can't live their life for them; they have such a different world. It's such a different world and it's so fast. A lot of it we don't know. I think it's good if kids are nice because a lot of things they talk about we don't know.

And even, I look at my life, my mother doesn't really. I mean, she's 82, she doesn't really. She's proud of me and she can read a newspaper and things like that, but in terms of the everyday, if I said the plane was an hour late, she would say, "Sugar, come on home." I mean, that's the way she thinks, you don't need to be bothered with that, baby come on home.

And I'll always, of course I love her anyway because she is always nice, I enjoy Mommy but you just want to keep putting that out. You don't have to be bothered, you just come on home, 'cause that's what your grandmother said, "Come on home, baby, if they don't treat you right, just come on home."

And that's all we can do and hope that they'll be all right, and hope that they have enough sense to keep us in mind, that they don't wait until that "Imitation of Life." You remember that crazy bitch running behind the casket, she was, "Momma, momma, I always loved you!" She's dead, you know, no, she was out of her mind, and her ambition was to be a dancer in Las Vegas; that's enough to kill you right there.

And so you gotta send her flowers while she is still alive. That's all you can do and you hope that the kids, and we do a lot for them, hopefully they understand that's all we were trying to do; it's still love. Didn't Toni Morrison say, "Love is always about the lover; crazy people love crazily, evil people love evilly"? And that's what she said and she's right; it's in *The Bluest Eye*.

Love is always about the lover and so what you trying do is the best you can. And there are things we don't know. We going to have kids that our grandchildren be half alien something, something from, son comes home with three-headed monster, "Mommy, this is Iola. She's from Jupiter," you know, 'cause black women are like "Come in, baby."

Black women accept anything, "Oh, yeah, she's nice, all them heads talk at the same time." That's the truth. We're easy enough to get along with. Things happen to us that we don't know what they're doing; we're just trying to say we're here. And if it gets to be too much, you just come on home. There's always a pot of beans or always some fried chicken. You come on home, because we love you anyway; just come on home. So I should go do something. So, thank you.

Nikki Giovanni

National Planner Jerry Ward, Jr.

Festival dancers

Congresswoman Corrine Brown

Jazz musician Jeff Rupert

Outdoor Festival

Main Stage audience

P.E.C.'s Sybil Pritchard and Cynthia Scales.

Zora Neale Hurston, Eatonville, and Black Self-Determination

Amiri Baraka

Amiri Baraka was a writer of poetry, drama, fiction, essays, and music criticism. He taught at the State University of New York at Buffalo and Stony Brook, Columbia University, and Rutgers University. While mainstream audiences consider much of Baraka's work controversial, he was one of the most respected African American writers of his generation. Amiri Baraka spoke at the sixteenth annual Zora Neale Hurston Festival of the Arts and Humanities in 2005, where he was introduced by Dr. Eleanor Traylor. Amiri Baraka died in January 2014, just a few weeks before he was to appear at the twenty fifth annual ZORA! Festival.

Eleanor Traylor:

The program committee has reminded us that "reunion" is the theme of this year's festival, and also requested that each of us state briefly why we feel that returning each year is important. I did, accordingly, submit an accurate, I think, and respectable, I hope, reason. What I did not say is that we need to come here every year because we have a ball. We see friends whom we'd like to see frequently but get to see only occasionally. We eat (and overeat) the most delicious food; I stopped and got my ribs before I came and sent them back so I'd be sure to have them. We shop the art of homegrown artists, and most of all we quench our thirst for conversations that we urgently need to hold together.

Those conversations were perhaps uppermost in the program committee's mind when it chose its theme of reunion for this year's festival and chose the panels that would explore it. But the composition of this panel stunned me. When the committee invited me to join a panel with the Barakas (Amiri and Amina) and Dr. [Richard A.] Long, I developed a fever blister, as I thought each of these could pleasurably keep us here all night. I was no less amazed when the committee asked that I submit a topic for discussion here. I thought each one of these was a topic. That's why I'll hurry. Nevertheless, what came to mind as a topic honoring the question of why we return to this festival annually and honoring each of these treasured speakers is the topic, "Zora is Home." The topic springs from a personal situation and from an historical one.

Persons who visit my mother's house in Atlanta, Georgia will notice that her living room features family pictures. Prominently displayed on adjacent walls as one enters the room are two poster-sized black-and-white photographs. One is a picture of me in Africa. The other is a picture of Ms. Hurston in that wonderful hat with the feather and that exquisite coat with the fur collar. You remember that one? It was not always the case that those pictures dominated my mother's living room. I found them there one time when I had returned home from one of my trips over the big horizon with Dr. Long and other members of his Center for the Study of African American Culture which he founded at Atlanta University. I shall never forget how I stood in awe before those pictures, remembering how my growing-up years in my mother's house had enacted the ceremony of reprimand and encouragement prefigured by Ms. Hurston in her story, "Drenched in Light," *Opportunity Magazine*, December 1924, repeated in *Jonah's Gourd Vine* and *Dust Tracks on a Road*.

No reader can ever forget those scenes where little icy Zora is reproached by her grandma: "Get down off of that gate post, you little sow. Looking them white folks right dead in their eye. They're gonna lynch you yet. Here, Joel, give me that wash stick.

I'll show that limb of Satan she can't shake herself at me. Get in this house, Madam."

Remembering such admonitions and not forgetting equal encouragements, I stood before the pictures thinking that often in my life I had wondered whether the people who "grew me up," as Ms. Hurston would say, thought that they had raised an idiot or worse. But on that day, I knew by those pictures that my mother had saluted me. The salute was not meant for achievement, no comparison intended with Ms. Hurston. The salute was for aspirations. To even aspire to be a woman like Zora Neale Hurston was sufficient to earn my mother's contentment. I remember saying to her as I stood before the pictures, "Oh, Ma," and she to me, "Yes, Mistress."

Since then, Zora Neale Hurston has been home for me. The historical reason why the Zora Neale Hurston Festival strikes me as home is that it fulfills, in large part, a request made by Ms. Hurston to Dr. [W. E. B.] DuBois in 1945. In that letter, which but for time would receive full recitation here, she asked Dr. DuBois, as Dean of Negro Orders, to propose a cemetery for the illustrious Negro dead. She said, "I feel strongly that the thing should be done. I think the lack of such a tangible thing allows our people to forget and their spirits evaporate."

We know that neither of Ms. Hurston's legendary dreams included the appearance of such persons of as N.Y., M.J., R.A., J.W., and all who have made an annual event celebrating her life possible. She who imagined splendid things had not imagined this festival. What she had thought of was a memorial place, something like Pere la Chez in Paris. I am quoting her, "A place where those who had widened the horizon and furthered the dream of the people, who, no matter what financial condition they might be in at death, would not lie in inconspicuous forgetfulness." She suggested to Dr. DuBois that the location of such a place be Florida because the vegetation would be green year round, because of the natural beauty of the state, and because thousands of acres are available and were as cheap as five to ten dollars an acre on lakes at the time. She suggested that this place would be a one-hundred-acre site to prevent white encroachment (she perhaps was thinking of our neighbors up the street) and besides it would afford space for an artist colony if the need arose. Ms. Hurston imagined this place of memory as a cemetery where, although their bones had long since gone to dust, one ought to see the tombs of Nat Turner, Frederick Douglass, and all the rest.

I suggest that as a geographical place, this festival, though not in scope, comes nearest to fulfilling Ms. Hurston's idea of a memorial home. As an idea, that home is one foremost accomplishment of contemporary African-American literature as it springs from Zora Neale Hurston's innovations in the production of narrative – home place, home speech, home agency, home critique, and home invention. In these ways, particularly and culturally, is Zora home to me.

In conclusion, and since I've been allowed this rather lengthy stay, I come to the festival with a desire. It is directed at the panel. I wish that Dr. Long now or before we leave this year's festival, would lead us in a discussion as to why Ms. Hurston's proposal to Dr. DuBois never received the table of consideration, not to speak of the table of implementation, and if those reasons may impact on ongoing possibilities of the Zora Festival. I wish in connection with the courtesy of Ms. Hurston's directions in the creative production and creative productions today that we could hear Amina Baraka read two sublime pieces of hers, one called "Being Colored" and the other called "Living is Hard." I brought them with me, but no one can read like her, and the conversation which would ensue from those two short pieces would be limitless but for time.

Finally, I wish that the foremost founding spirit of the Black Arts movement, if you date it from the 1960s, [Amiri Baraka], would read his poem "In the Tradition." If he says he does not have it with him, I have brought it. The poem should be heard on all occasions that concern us, and all occasions do. There is a line in that poem that reads something like, "Cut me and Zora Neale and a bunch of others in half," so and so. If we could unpack that line, we would be here all night, pleasurably. It's such a joy to see you. Thank you.

N. Y. Nathiri:

Well, thank you, Dr. Traylor, for that opening statement, and we move directly on to Amiri Baraka who may or may not read the poem at this moment, but will respond, I'm sure to what Dr. Traylor has said.

Amiri Baraka:

Well, I thought she was just started. I don't know why you stopped. Well, let me do what I can do. I thought that what Ella [Traylor] was doing was very, very enlightening for me. But let me say this: Zora Neale, Eatonville, Reconstruction. Those things, first of all, should tell you something. Eatonville's surrounded now by Disney World. See, that should tell you what's happening. Black self-determination confused with independence. There's a difference. Self-determination, which is what we have to do still, self-determination.

And, see, what Zora later did not understand and what DuBois understood later, you understand, is what our missing link is. When he says the double consciousness, you know, to see yourself always through the eyes of people that hate you, to look at yourself with that mixture of amusement and contempt, that's like a Spike Lee movie, but the question first of being black, we understand that except if we need some kind of real therapy, which we have to give every once in a while. That's what the Black Arts movement is. That's what the Harlem Renaissance was. It's the therapy, you know, to re-endarken yourself as to who you is, but that should be a given.

On the other side, the question of being an American, it's always in contention. You understand, we're still fighting that battle. What do I mean, being an American? I mean equal rights, you know what I'm saying? Democracy. Now some people want to call their self Africans. That's cool. I asked a brother one time, he said, "Why you don't want to call yourself an African?" I said, "Where you from, brother?" He said, "Ghana." I said, "I'm an Afro-American. See, what you want to do is diminish my nationality. You understand, my nationality, I'm a Black American." Whether you like it or not. You born here. Go to Africa, you'll find out you're an American, quick.

So the question of the double consciousness is the struggle for equal rights on one hand and the struggle for self-determination on the other. You got two hands for that reason. Now Zora coming out of Eatonville, reconstruction, a black city where they confuse self-determination with independence, you understand, we ain't no colony. You could not be independent in America. See, Disney World would grow around you and they will elect one of his characters as the President, you see, so then the question of that need for self-determination and democratic struggle, that's the double-edged sword.

Now, on one hand, democracy. We are Americans, we have to struggle for anything that Americans got to accept their stupidity. Everything. You got a house, I want a house. You got a education, I want a education. You got a job, I want a job. You live in a good neighborhood, I want to live in a good neighborhood. But on the other hand, we cannot wait for some revelation of humanity to come to people who brought us here in the bottom of a boat. You must at the same time strive to get what you want to, even if it is creating a weapon to facilitate getting it.

So those are the two sides of that. And that's why, later on, Zora Neale rejected FEPC, 'cause she thought it was begging. She didn't understand it was democratic struggle, you see. When she gives that statement, what was it she called it, weeping about being "I am no, the Negro, oh I am so," remember, what did she call it? She had a name for them. She said, "I am not no weeping Negro. I come here to pop this sucker." Well, you play Zora Neale. You supposed to talk about that. What did she say? She said, "I did not come here weeping and whining. I come to bust this open." That's that question of self-determination. She full of that, you see. But she confused self-determination with complete independence.

We are not a colony. We are Americans, and so we have that double-edged sword. That is the struggle for equality, for equal rights, democratic rights, but at the same time to fight for self-determination, the right to do what we need to do, you see, so that, you know, the boys of course learn from [Marcus] Garvey later. Garvey and the boys fighting that. That's what they was fighting about. Malcolm X and Elijah Muhammad, that's what they was fighting about. Self-determination versus democratic rights.

And so then somebody codifies it and calcifies it into segregation versus integration. That's lies, that's lies, that's a lie. That's a jive contradiction. You understand, what we want is self-determination and equal rights. We are American citizens who've never been given that equality of citizenship, but we know we black and we have something to do to get that. Let me say some other things so that we know Garvey and the boys would have been better in a united front. Let them fight all day and all night, like they do in the Congress of the United States. They fight. They say, "I don't agree with that, but that's the law."

Malcolm X and Elijah Muhammad, same thing. One arm over here, one arm over there. Those are two different struggles. The struggle in the South and the struggle in the North are two different struggles. What Malcolm was talking about and what Martin Luther King was talking about, those are two different struggles. We should have been sitting together at the table. I saw Malcolm a month before he died, and he told me the same thing: "united front." I saw Martin Luther King seven days before he died, he came to my house in Newark, knocked on the door. "Hello, Leroi. You don't look like such a bad person. People told me you was a bad person." That's what Dr. Martin Luther King said. "I ain't no bad person, Dr. King." But he told me the same thing, he told me, "united front." Both of them, Malcolm X and Martin Luther King. Would that they had both understood that clearly before they both got iced. Would that DuBois and Garvey both understood that clearly before they both got iced, you understand what I'm saying? What am I saying?

Let me get back to the literary part of it. The brilliance of Zora: *Mule Bone*. One of those great plays of our time. Why was it obscured? Because middle class Negroes couldn't stand to go back to the country and hear that language, some of the most beautiful language of the world coming out of they mouths, you understand, what was they fighting over, whether they should have a jail or not. I mean, that's the extent of that kind of contradiction. I mean, the Baptists say we don't need no jail, if we get a jail, we'll get somebody to put in it. But *Mule Bone* and the life story, Zora Neale story, you know what I mean, that was a mistake all the way around, I mean.

But still the short stories, "The Skillet," the great novel, *Their Eyes Were Watching God* and the way she deals with those three prototypes of Negro men, is that precise or not? The patriarchy of the country, old man he smell like dead stuff, she gotta get away from him, she go meet Joe. Then the more developed male chauvinism of petty capitalism, still tied to the patriarchy, but developed just an inch little more there. And then her sexual love with my man, which she got from my Haitian experience, which finally gets ruined by what, a mad dog chauvinism, mad slobbering dog bites her and then she come back needs a chicken and chow, like my wife said, long travels, talking 'bout the world.

That's Zora Neale. She's a brilliant woman, the sanctified church, *Their Eyes Were Watching God*; oh, if you wanna see, if you wanna hear that, listen to Ruby Dee's version of that, she does a CD where she plays all the parts, or listen to that child right there, plays a pretty good Zora Neale right there. The sanctified church where she talks about black styles, aesthetics, the whole question of our language, the question of dynamics, the form, why you like things sideways, why you hate a straight line, why you still talk the same language that you talked ten thousand years ago, like you say Oedipus was, what, a "lame," Oedipus he had a club foot which still that's lame, he copulated with his mama, you know we always talking about that, "blah, blah, blah." Interesting that "mufuh" is the same as the Swahili word "mafah," which means Holocaust, and I ain't never heard a Negro say, "mother" except myself. Most of them say "mufuh," you know they say it just like it is.

The angle of success is like a pyramid in Egypt. The angle of failure is a square, a lame square. That's why she's such a great anthropologist, because she checks out the aesthetic of the people. You check her language and talking 'bout two pimps talking 'bout a Black Russian. He's a "black rushin'," rushing up here from Georgia last week. She's on it. And then, "Tell My Heart" is a study of mores in Haiti, you know, Baron Samedi. Brilliant cultural anthropologist, researcher, particularly a cultural analyst of style, of aesthetics, of mores, of so-called Black language, it's always alive, always in motion.

People who want to talk about standard English are trying to keep a job. People talking 'bout Ebonics are trying to get one. Of course, the language changes momentarily. You understand we never spoke Standard English. George Washington beat them people way back there. Most of these white people come from where? Ireland, Wales, Scotland. They ain't never spoke English neither. We know we never spoke English. And, let me see. On and on and on and on and on.

Woman question. There are very few people who deal with the woman question as finely as Zora Neale. And so, you know, I would just send that, first of all, Zora Neale being obscure is a result of national oppression. No black author that has all their books published and in print, none, neither Langston (Hughes), nor DuBois. You can get a copy of DuBois if you pay fourteen hundred dollars to a Communist group in Massachussetts. I've been threatening to get that for a long time. But you cannot like you would get a Henry James. Now, but even progressive literature, you cannot get Herman Melville, look for the complete works of Mark Twain. I have twelve books published from William Morrow. Ten are out of print. See, I'm just trying to tell you something.

But, on the other hand, when they could put her down for being a self-segregationist, Zora confused self-determination. She understood self-determination. What they called black pride: pride ain't enough. You gotta have something. We are people with fifty million people, okay maybe forty million people, more than most of the nations of the United Nations with a national product of 500 billion dollars a year. We are the sixteenth largest gross national product in the world. Fifteenth is General Motors. This is the World Bank. They gotta know so they can get their hand in your pocket.

So what she says there, the question of self-determination, that's real. We wouldn't be able to put together a stable national political organization, like we tried to do in 1845, like we tried to do in 1941, like we tried to do in 1972, over and over again, not because we separate from America, but because we in it. But we have to have somebody that we done elected democratically, we have to tell what can we do with that $500 billion dollars a year, what can we do with it, you understand? Thank you.

This poem came out, let me qualify it, '82. It was written in the late 70s. Don't qualify it? "In the Tradition." Now I want to ask Dr. Traylor what her response to that is since she provoked it.

Eleanor Traylor:
My response is this: That poem has been on my mind since it was written. I have been trying to persuade the Department of English at Howard to rename it in the name of Sterling Allen Brown, to rename it in the tradition of "In the Tradition," and for twelve years I have struggled, we have struggled, in that department to raise a Chair in his name, an endowed Chair. We have raised, this is a little academic department, you know, so far, in twelve years, a half million dollars. I don't think I can live long enough to raise the other half. You know it takes a million or a little bit more to fully endow a Chair, and I've been holding fish fries, this and that, everything, to get the little money to get there. Why is that? That was his English professor. And that was the man who commended Ms. Hurston, you know, to the wide world of literature.

So the question Ms. Hurston raised that I want Dr. Long to address is a question very similar to that. Why can't we name things their true names, for one thing. Why has it taken forever to

endow a Chair in the name of the man [Sterling Brown] who was
the pioneer of the study of African-American literature in the
Academy? Why was the cemetery or something like that never
implemented? And do those reasons have anything to do with the
ongoing nature of a memorial like this festival? I just want to hear
from the occult some possible answers.

Richard A. Long:

Well, first of all, I can't answer that. But I suppose I could
indulge in some brief speculation, and it does come close to this
whole idea of tradition. We are a spiritual people, and we tend to
couch our expectations in terms which are aligned to what we
identify as spiritual, namely the biblical, the religious, and so on. I
think our problem is to redirect that energy for the spiritual, that
spiritual energy, into some appreciation of our humanity, and
therefore of our heroes, and we simply haven't gotten there.

I'm not even sure that we're on the path, but I think that the
kind of thing that you are doing in raising a question of a Chair to
be named for Sterling Brown, whom I knew, as he was your
colleague at Howard, wasn't he? He was a professor of Amiri
Baraka and Toni Morrison and several people in this room were
students of his, and I think that we haven't harnessed our current
engines of publicity to the task. So you've been struggling and
working there at Howard, but the word has not really gotten out.
And I think that here, what has happened with this festival, the
word has gotten out because a tremendous amount of energy was
generated in the process and so on, and it does come back to Zora
Neale Hurston's project of memorializing.

I don't think, as DuBois did not think, that we need a
cemetery, but we do need that particular kind of active inventory
of achievement. We need a spiritual cemetery. We need a
cemetery of the imagination, a cemetery of the mind. There's a
great deal, I think, of connection between her discourse, her
question to DuBois, his inability to answer, his indisposition to
answer, and so on, but there's a tremendous amount of energy in

the African-American community which goes to the support of, to the extension of, things which are really not terribly important.

Amiri Baraka:

Can I say something? First of all, that's what I was talking about. Sterling Brown was my English professor. I didn't even know who he was. He came to us one time and said, you know, "You all think you all hip," because the berets, we had heard Charlie Parker. He said, "Come to my house." This is when Howard University had band jazz on its campus. This black university had band jazz on its campus. Sterling took us to his house, and we went in this room he had, and he showed us this wall of black music by genre, chronology, and artist. He said to us one thing: he said, "That's your history."

Took me a decade to put that together. That's where the book *Blues People* come from. I did not understand, I knew what the words was, but I didn't know he was telling you that is your history. Study it up, study that music. When the people change, the music changes. You analyze the lyrics and the style, you can tell where they was, what they was doing, time, place, and condition, you see, now he had to teach that in his house. He had to teach that in Cook Hall in the dormitory in the evenings. Why?

And I could name a whole lot of other crazy Negroes was there who tried to enforce that. When Jimmy Baldwin's play came to Howard, *The Amen Corner*, dude told us that would set the Speech Department back many years. My famous incident about eating the watermelon on the campus, but that split between the struggle for democracy, which some people think, we just want to be in this. Talk to a Condoleezza Rice. Talk to a Clarence Thomas, they just want to be in this.

Now, I ain't got no other connection with nothing. Even if your struggle put them where they are. Ain't no black person got nowhere by their self. You understand? So you got that still, you got that struggle. You got Negroes talking about they want to be Africans, they don't want to be Black Americans. Well, what you doing over here, then? Still chained to slavery. "We was a slave!"

That is not on me. That's on slave takers and masters, you see, so you got that split between people struggling only for equal rights and DuBois suffering from that and only from that and that question first until that's why he said "double consciousness" until he understood. And he understood after he had that struggle with Garvey.

Then the later Dubois in the '30s started talking about the nation within the nation, you understand? And about how we have to use segregation as a strength since we have our own marketing association. Just the question is: the double consciousness has not been resolved as one thing. We are one people. Yeah, we got a schizophated, bifurcated mentality, but you have to use that. You can't run away from yourself. You're still yourself. You understand? I mean, Condoleezza said, "We did not have to have a civil rights movement, they let my parents in the stores on Sundays." Is that what it was about? Bush said the other day, "Y'all should be in favor of us privatizing Social Security because y'all die early anyway." My God. So that psychological, historical split, house Negro, field Negro, that Malcolm talk about, Dubois when he got rid of that talented tenth idea because he saw the selfishness of the black bourgeois. You know, read this stuff.

That becomes, then, consolidated into class, I mean you can see the struggle between [Alain] Locke and DuBois. You can see the struggle between Claude McKay and DuBois. McKay said, "You don't know nothing 'bout no art, Doctor, you know about propaganda." DuBois said, "I don't give a damn about art that ain't propaganda." That's struggle. But then in the 60s, that gets solidified. Why? Because that pimple of development that the people who got killed, who got locked up, who got their heads split open, their teeth knocked out, those who would never go to college, allowed that pimple worth of Negroes to consolidate – psychological bifurcation, you understand?

So there became a material bifurcation. So there became real class alienation and real class struggle but the woman got on a costume. Somebody said, "That's a black woman, ain't that a shame?" That ain't a black woman, that's the Secretary of State. You understand what I'm saying? That's the Secretary of State. I don't care what you see. That's the Secretary of State. And for you that say, "That's a black woman, ain't that a shame?" You better get that out your mind.

And so, let me try to sum up. Nixon actually pulled the policy thing that did that, see, he killed us, the militants, locked us up, some still locked up, and at the same time, put out black capitalism. So you see the brilliance of that, where there was a mass movement, wooh, right down the middle. Y'all go to jail, y'all get black capitalism. And now the heirs of black capitalism are the Negroes we see running around, y'all talking about "oh, we got."

And finally, when you say the church, I agree with you. Think about this, like self-determination and how Bush got to the church before we did. In Newark, there are 52 Baptist churches in the phone book. I ain't talking about in the cellar, upstairs, round the back, 52 Baptist churches in the phone book. Not talking 'bout Methodist or no other weird-ass churches you got, but I'm talking 'bout Baptist. I'm talking about 52 in a community of less than 300,000 people. Now how do they sustain that? Theater, people, how do you sustain that? You mean to tell me, y'all can't have 50 theaters? You mean to tell me you got 27 cities where you are the plurality and the majority and you can't have one theater per city? Why not? Because you'd rather go to Hollywood.

That's one side of it. Only equality, not equal rights, not self-determination. They would rather make white chicks than have a storefront theater for 50 people. You understand, that's the mentality. Because we have the wealth to do whatever we want. Five hundred billion dollars, you can do anything you want. Fifty million people, you can do anything you decide to do and everybody gonna get out your way, you understand that? Understanding that is the question.

I accept these two informed answers, you know, I mean crisis in consciousness, crack in consciousness, and embryonism in consciousness. But let me just say this: these two raised enough people. This one called the likes of Jerry Ward and the rest of us in here to consciousness, and if you want to be blacks, then you should assume the scholarship of your people. That's what we commenced to do. And Jerry and I raised quite a number. This man raised a number of folks all over the world. Those are enough. We are a spiritual people, but ain't nobody more spiritual than me and Jerry, understand what I mean?

And using that spirituality as a conductor to something else. I want to get to the last point that Man is money. Spirituality does not preclude money. Spirituality is connected to means and resources to bring about what you love most in the world. That's what it's about. We do not so much what we think and reason about. We do what we love. All these people have raised enough people to do that Chair, to do that young woman's bookstore, we are not alone in this.

There is a collaborative consciousness at work. We wouldn't be alive if there weren't. If we hadn't loved one another, we wouldn't be alive to survive those ships, to survive this recent calamity. It has taken its toll on me, everybody can see I've got fever blisters, can't hardly get myself, but I'm here, don't let nobody turn me round. If you want to do it, you can do it. We have enough. Mr. DuBois said we never had an army. Now I don't know why Mr. DuBois didn't get on the army of that project because we realize that Ms. Hurston said cemetery, but you know what she talking about. That people who have widened the horizons and implemented the dreams of a people. What is it Ms. [Harriet] Tubman said? "I have known the applause of multitudes. Your only witnesses are the moon and the midnight stars. If it weren't for you, nothing." That's when they asked Mr. [Frederick] Douglass to authenticate, and he said, "That's impossible. That is an impossibility. It is she who authenticates me, not the other way around."

The thing is, there was never an army. There were always enough. We can do it. I accept the answer that perhaps publicity is the media, people know about what they want to know about, you know what I'm saying? Look at these tabloids and things. All that stuff, all that horror that they put before, suddenly it gets out, everybody knows about it. This is a wonderful thing. It's called *The Black Quarterly*. It's coming out of Stanford these days. Somebody asked me if the British government couldn't send a black writer of its selection to the English Department and, like a reflex, I said no, and they said, "This is a great opportunity." I said, "The voice of the government, and the voice of a poet are two different voices." To prove that, a government recently hung a poet in Nigeria. Another government, who had awarded a Poet Laureateship to a poet of the world wanted to retract it when the poet wrote something that the government didn't like. So I said, "No, not under my watch!" I don't expect any broadening experience; you get it.

But now my original point. I didn't mean to go into all that, but let it herefore be publicized that we need to endow a Chair for the man who gave the first course in African-American literature in the Academy and raised contemporary literature because contemporary literature is African-American literature. You know it, the whole world knows it. Everybody is writing like that. So that's something we love, don't we? We love this festival, and the point I was making was, can the festival get enough money to make sure it can sustain itself from year to year? I hope so. I hope it doesn't got to go begging like me. I never thought I had to be a beggar. I just thought I had to teach. No, no you have to go out and, you see what I'm saying?

The question is that we have a treasure chest, you know, and there is no richer literature in the world than African-American literature. There's no richer art, there's no richer music. Everything in the United States, and I would say the world, is pimped off your back, you understand? Somebody talking about rock'n'roll. Rock'n'roll? What's that? You understand what I'm saying? The American language. The point is that if we know that and we are not these crazy Negroes going around saying, "Oh no, I ain't never eat no greens, I don't know nothing about black eyed peas." Now you know good and well that the black bourgeois would be the most vicious people in the world if they would see you eating that fried chicken before Popeye got there.

You got the treasure chest. Now, they'd rather do House Party 12, Boyz n the Hood 35. Here's Spike doing all of this, no I ain't going to call a name, but here's people doing all of this garbage, but has anybody tried to do the works of Langston Hughes? Has anybody tried to do *Their Eyes Were Watching God*? They say they're going to do it. God knows they did the Charlie Parker story, now we know that had to be done again. They did the Billie Holiday story, we know that had to be done again. But where's the Louis Armstrong story? Where's the Fred Douglass story? Where's the complete work of the slave narratives, of the escaped slaves? Where's the Nat Turner story? You think the Boys n the Hood is exciting? Put Fred Douglass on film. Make a musical of that July 5th speech. Come on with it. You bad. Do it. Y'all Negroes walking around in the movies. Do that. Morgan Freeman, do that. Ice Cube, do that. Instead of you running around talking bad about Martin Luther King and Rosa Parks, don't you know, Negro, if it wasn't for Martin Luther King and Rosa Parks, you'd be in a real barber shop. Wouldn't be no movie, you'd be cutting hair. You understand what I'm saying?

So the question is, here you sitting around with 500 billion dollars, what's wrong with you. "I ain't got no money, don't nobody love me." Got 50 million people with 500 billion dollars, what else you need? I'll finish with the one problem is, you say, spiritual. Negroes old. See, I got a poem I'm going to read one day about old-ass Negroes. What do I mean by that? They old. I mean, in other words, like Langston. I got that from Langston, nobody couldn't treat you like this if you wasn't so old. You know what I mean, Negroes sit up in the chair, sing, "mah Lord," and you say, "What is that?" When they stop that, they go kick somebody's ass.

You understand what I'm saying? They not quick to anger. They gonna be gone. We were slaves for a thousand years to people that looked like us. Like them people in Australia, what they call them, the Aborigines? They don't even believe there's such a place as Australia. I was talking to an Aborigine, I said, "You from Australia?" He said, "There's no such a place as Australia." "It's on the map!" "That ain't real, bro."

You talk about dream time, that's in your mind. It's on your back too, I'll bet you that. But I'm saying that kind of consciousness, look how slow they walk, been here, did that. Like DuBois said about the Sisyphus Syndrome, you roll a rock up that mountain and roll it down on your head. I'm saying we need a culture revolution, you artists, all of that treasure chest of ours got to be put to work. Look at the bestseller list. Is anything there you can remember thirty years from now? Look at the flicks. Look at Broadway. It's the culture of a people about to get out of bed. It's a death culture. Look at the movies. Go to the movies. Who gonna win the Oscars? Armenia and I went to see *The Aviator*. That's the worst flick I seen. It's gonna win everything. What is it about? A billionaire who go crazy. That's interesting. Well, Hotel Rwanda, with a boy fighting to save people lives. That ain't interesting. It's some colored stuff. It's the culture of these people which we would rather accept to be part of, see that black exploitation film. They discovered we don't need to do an all-black film, all we need to do is put one Negro in the film, no matter how jive it is, and they'll show up. They'll start building their own thing. Don't let me go on and on. I will.

Writer Amiri Baraka

Writer Amiri Baraka

Eatonville quilters

Smooth jazz artist Najee (right)

Bethune Cookman College Choir

Young festival dancers.

Anthropologist and Educator
Johnetta Cole
on Zora Neale Hurston

Johnetta B. Cole is a distinguished educator, cultural anthropologist, and humanitarian. She was the first female president of Spelman College from 1987 to 1997, and president of Bennett College from 2002 to 2007. Dr. Cole is currently director of the Smithsonian Institution's National Museum of African Art. She spoke at the sixteenth annual Zora Neale Hurston Festival of the Arts and Humanities in 2005, and was introduced by Harriett L. Elam-Thomas, Ambassador-in-Residence at the University of Central Florida.

N. Y. Nathiri:

It is my pleasure to welcome you to the annual Zora Neale Hurston Arts and Humanities lecture. This culturally pivotal event is underwritten by Hillsborough Community College, Seminole Community College, Rollins College, and the University of Central Florida. This occasion signifies the height of the needed social, historical, cultural, and intellectual response to the challenges and opportunities of today's global community, particularly in the world of academia. It is my privilege to present at this time the honorable Harriet Edam Thomas, Ambassador in Residence, University of Central Florida. Thank you.

Harriett L. Elam-Thomas:

A special "Good morning" to you all.

The dates: January 13 through 15, 1994.

The place: MIT's Kresge Auditorium in Cambridge, Massachusetts.

The event: Black Women in the Academy: Defending our Name - 1894 to 1994.

The speaker: Dr. Johnetta Cole.

The impact: lasting.

The date: February 16, 1995.

The place: Spelman College, Atlanta, Georgia.

The event: My courtesy call on then president, Johnetta Cole, of Spelman College.

The greeting: What is now considered Dr. Cole's signature greeting, "Welcome, Sister Ambassador." Was that greeting clairvoyant? Remember, this was 1994.

The impact: phenomenal, for four years later I was actually sworn in as the US Ambassador to Senegal.

Now those are just two of several occasions during which I have had the joy, blessing, and privilege to be in the presence of Dr. Cole. It was, however, the first occasion, in 1994, that had, indeed, a lasting impact, for I had just returned from four years in Istanbul, Turkey. When I walked into that MIT auditorium and saw some 2,015 women of color from all over the United States, including Hawaii and Alaska, I was moved to tears. I listened to Lani Guinier, Angela Davis, cover a wide spectrum of our country's contribution to the academy. I thought I had heard it all until Dr. Cole spoke. I knew then I was in the presence of one of the world's premier anthropologists and civic activists. I am certain the students at Spelman College, and now those at Bennett College, recognize how blessed they are to have been touched by the intellectual brilliance, social consciousness, cultural sensitivity, and genuine commitment to the education of women of Dr. Johnetta B. Cole. What makes today's task even more exhilarating and more exciting for me is that she belongs to yet another sisterhood with which I am also affiliated - she doesn't know this until now - Delta Sigma Theta Sorority. You have in your program highlights of what we would all agree is a riveting chronicle of Dr. Cole's selfless sharing of her God-given gift with others. So please join me in welcoming America's true Sister President, Dr. Johnetta B. Cole.

Johnetta Cole:

My Sister Ambassador delivered a wonderful introduction for which I am so grateful. To my sisters and my brothers all, "Good morning." Seated as you are, and standing as I am, in a sacred place, I move to say that this is a great "gittin' upon."

What a joy it is for me. What a joy it is to come and be a part of a festival, of a movement, that bears the name of one of my 'sheroes'. Usually, out of respect for someone who has done a great deal of work, good work, I would never use only a first name. But for all of us now, there is not only respect but love and affection, and so we say of her, "Zora!" I come to you from one of only two historically black colleges for women. Spelman, as you know, is in Atlanta, Georgia. And I now have the privilege of working at Bennett College for Women. It is such a treat for me to come in to be greeted first by my Spelman sisters, and then by my Bennett sisters. But I want to turn to all of you and say thank you for giving me this privilege of offering these words in actually a rather formal lecture; something I don't often do. But I do this today out of a deep need to capture my views and emotions and my intellectual wrestling with the life of Zora Neale Hurston. I also feel a sense of responsibility to speak in general to all of the women of those two institutions, Bennett and Spelman, and, indeed, to all women, as W. E.B. DuBois would call them, Sister Ambassador, "women of the darker hue."

But in going out in concentric circles as we must, living as we do in a global village, I respectfully dare to speak in the interests of all women. As many of you may know, I am trained formally as an anthropologist. And so as a young student and then as a more mature professor and scholar, to whom could I look? Of course, to

Ruth Benedict, of course, to Margaret Meade, but I could also look to Zora Neale Hurston, with her incredibly irreverent self. Who received her degree in Anthropology and was known to have stood on street corners in Harlem with her instruments measuring people's heads, though we know her best for managing to get inside of people's heads and hearts and souls. And so I offer you now, this talk which I have titled, 'Zora Neale Hurston: Wolf Woman Singing over the Bones'.

In Mexico they tell the story of La Loba, the wild woman whose purpose in life is the collection of bones. According to Clarissa [Pinkola Estes] she is known to collect and preserve especially that which is in danger of being lost in the world. Once La Loba collects the bones she sings over them until the creature's bones are once again fleshed out and alive. Associated especially with wolves, La Loba the wild woman has a double meaning. La Loba is the wild woman in a creature related to the wolves. As the wolf she has sprung into being vanishes into the canyon, she is transformed into a laughing woman who runs free. Zora Neale Hurston is a direct descendant of La Loba. An anthropologist who collected the bones of African-American folklore, an artist with words who has sung over these bones and made them live again. And a laughing woman who refused to submit her soul and her personality to the conventions of her time. Yes, our sister Zora experienced the solitary journey of La Loba.

Hurston did not enjoy total acceptance from her critics, either in her lifetime or in the ten years following her death. She had been called everything - and rarely a Child of God - everything from a sacrificing genius to a handkerchief-head nigger. Her personality and behavior were more important to her critics than her work until 1977, when Robert Hemenway published Zora Neale Hurston's literary biography. In recognizing her genius, he was the first critic who was indignant that she had ended her life in obscurity and poverty. This woman, who was folklorist, novelist, anthropologist, journalist, and critic, inspired both extreme dislike and extreme admiration. Darwin Turner has called her "quick-tempered, arrogant, obsequious, and desperate." Then let us remind him that a single black woman, with no visible income except that meager amount which her writing was bringing in, was probably desperate enough to do whatever she had to in order to work and to eat.

According to our sister "shero" Alice Walker, the assessment of Hurston's work has been inadequate, sometimes venomous, and often highly improper. I suggest that it was Zora's refusal to suppress the wild woman she was that made so many uncomfortable women dislike her and yet, of course, made others admire her. I suggest that it was her feminist's, womanist's, self that so offended many and led to the misreading of her outstanding contribution to scholarship and literature. Zora is La Loba. She collects bones and sings over them until they spring to life once more and, as such, is always on the fringes of polite society, where magic women have always been. Like Pilate in Toni Morrison's *Song of Solomon*, who is also carrying around a bag of bones, Zora too is gifted, or cursed, with the ability to see where others are blind. And thus she becomes a threat to so many. Zora herself wrote that discovering the ability to have psychic vision as a 7-year-old ended her childhood. The writer [Clarissa Pinkola] Estes says, "Both healthy wolves and healthy women share certain psychic characteristics in that both have been hounded, harassed, and falsely imputed to be devouring, overly aggressive, and of less value than those who are their detractors."

The political issues of race that were so prominently in the minds of writers of the Harlem Renaissance created a dilemma for Hurston, who refused to be openly militant. And yes, those of us who were children of the 60s may well want to remake Zora Neale Hurston in our own image. But we dare not. It is our responsibility to respect the integrity of who she was. Langtson Hughes and Arna Bontemps both suggested that Hurston assumed a road designed to gain the assistance of white people. In fact, Arna Bontemps wrote to many of his white friends, "No doubt, she was a perfect darkie, in the nice meaning they give the term. That is, a naïve, childlike, sweet, humorous and highly-colored Negro." One wonders if any of Zora Neale Hurston's male colleagues ever thought about what options were open to them as men that were not open to a single woman who wanted to live freely as an artist. Zora Neale Hurston wanted to live free as an artist. Darwin Turner also represents her as a person inclined to play the fool for whites and then goes on to make reference to her conflicts with her sister, her brother, and her mother-in law. Well, yeah, there was family conflict. Anybody in here without a little family drama? He then cites an incident in which Hurston alleged that a northern Negro organization was enticing Negroes to vote as a block by promising them Cadillacs, sheets, and towels. He writes, "Even if she believed that anyone would naively expect to receive a Cadillac or its monetary equivalent for a single vote she would have damaged her reputation for intelligence less if she had limited her allegations to sheets and towels. Clearly, Mr. Turner has a limited understanding of satire and the use of hyperbole so often associated with folklore. And Zora was steeped in folklore. He also appears to have no sense of humor. He gives no positive assessment of her contribution and overlooks what must be finally noticed. And that is that Zora Neale Hurston was an outstanding novelist, a skilled folklorist, and a prolific writer; in fact, for 30 years, the most prolific black writer in America as an anthropologist. Yes, she was eccentric.

But I am struck as I read so much about what was said about her. I am struck by the glaring class prejudice and sexism. Here was a woman with the double jeopardy known by all woman of color. And a woman who, indeed, was never privileged to have material wealth and so, yes, race, gender, and class were her jeopardies. How was she to live on her writing? Who besides Langston Hughes had become successful enough to become financially independent? In the 30s, the 40s, and the 50s, a woman who chose a career, and especially a single life, also chose poverty as well. Turner, for example, failed to mention that as Zora Neale

Hurston worked as a cook and a maid she was also working on *Moses, Man of the Mountain*. Until the 1960s feminist movement blossomed, a woman who refused to compromise her work was looked upon as freakish and even immoral. And the whole force of society came down upon her to impose the traditional female role model which Hurston would have nothing of. She was a high-energy person capable of intense work and personal effervescence and she frequently overwhelmed people. Her refusal to be anything except herself was threatening to critics and, certainly, to male critics who wrote about her. She refused to believe there was anything wrong with her. And although she avoided confrontation on the race question, in my view, she spent her life trying to contribute to the preservation of black culture. Alice Walker has written, "Zora was a cultural revolutionary simply because she was herself."

My eyes just met with a great brother scholar, Richard Long. Brother Richard Long, you know this. You know what it means to be a cultural revolutionary, simply because you are one yourself. Without money of one's own in a capitalist society, Alice Walker says, there is no such thing as financial independence. It is not as though the male writers of the Harlem Renaissance did not take white money. Out great Langston Hughes, himself, was for two years supported by Godmother Charlotte Mason. Although Zora received favorable press from the New York Times and the New York Herald for her now classic work, *Their Eyes Were Watching God*, I'm thinking Richard Wright entirely missed the point of the novel and thought she was advancing a minstrel image. He said, "Writing about a black woman's internal life did not help race matters. The sensory sweep of her novel carries no theme, no message, no thought." And so Richard Wright, with all of our gratitude for his monumental literary work, has, with one swipe of a sentence, declared that a black woman's internal life has no validity or importance. As if this internal life is not reflective of the reality of race matters, which of course, affect her life.

Locke also chided her for not coming to grips with motive fiction and social document fiction. But if you read Hurston with different eyes, perhaps a woman's eye or the eyes of a righteously conscious man, then you know she is writing protest literature, as when she writes about the soul-killing effects of marriage, not on all but on many women. In Janie, our central sister in *Their Eyes Were Watching God*, Zora created a character that finally succeeded in knowing her own mind. But she also created a character, not only here but in other places, who reveals to us, my sisters, our capacity to participate in our own oppression. Valerie Boyd, to whom we are all grateful for her work on Zora Neale Hurston, has said that, "Hurston raised critical questions concerning the intimidation and oppression inherent in too many relationships." And she challenged black men and everyone else to listen and then to act and to do accordingly. Boyd said that Hurston seems to say that marriage is a deadly proposition in which someone has to give up his or her life. And in most cases, it would be the woman. In Zora's work, *Sweat*, Delia chooses her own life, however, over the life of her cruel husband. I think white oppression was also present in the events that unfold in *Their Eyes Were Watching God*. A little white oppression is actually in many of Hurston's stories. But it is most fundamentally wrapped and intertwined in a woman's internal journey; a woman's internal journey which, of course, was about race. Zora was simply not afraid to be powerful, to be daring, to be different, to be authentic - in other words, to be her own bad self. A young writer, Richard Bruce Nugent, says, and I love these words, "Zora would have been Zora if she had been an Eskimo." Zora said of herself, "Even as a child, one of the most serious objections to me was that, having nothing, I still did not know how to be humble." The wild woman was alive in the wild child. In the Mexican tradition that I have referenced, the wolf, the wolf woman, the wild woman, represents a kind of instinctual knowing, straddling the past and the future simultaneously. Certainly the anthropologist in Zora made a magnificent attempt to know both the past and the present by collecting tales that would otherwise have been lost to time, therefore propelling the present and the past into the future. And she didn't stop there but, by singing this culture into the present time, she makes it live again and again and again for us in her novels and stories.

A passage that I remember and love so well is the one in which Zora Neale Hurston, collecting folktales, describes how someone properly eats fish and sucks the bones. It's the description, when we aren't trying to be High Society, that is as relevant today as when her keen ethnographic pen described it.

Toni Cade Bambara in 1981 wrote this of Zora, "The woman would not behave." She had a mission, knew what her work in the world was, and she pursued it. It's clear that Zora Neale Hurston was on the cutting edge with her work, blending the boundaries between literature and anthropology, between fiction and ethnology. She was ahead of her time in terms of placing folkloric texts in context and demonstrating the process of their creation as part of a lived culture. She was on the cutting edge with her own life refusing the expectation of both white and black middle class America.

Zora scandalized North Carolina College in Durham. By doing what? Wearing trousers and a man's fedora. She pretended she was a bootlegger's girlfriend on the lam. She sang work songs with me. She was initiated into voodoo. This was not ladylike behavior for those times; this was not ladylike behavior for any time. But it didn't worry Zora. The important thing was to get the stories, get the songs that people had to offer. She paid a price in her personal life for her unwavering devotion to her work. Zora was married and divorced three times to men who could not understand that her work was more of a priority to her than being a traditional wife. The most compelling arguments for Zora as a feminist (a feminist is simply one who believes that women and men are created equal) are found in her own life's journey. She refused to let those three marriages change the way she moved through the world. Her mother had been a role model for her. She said her mother was the one to dare all, while her father was satisfied with things as they were.

Although Zora created stories of women who were living or were attempting to live as subordinate wives, these women often triumphed over oppression. Now I am sure, or at least I suspect, that Zora would have denied the label of feminist or womanist and certainly she would not want to be known as a race woman. But she did address the problem of black identity in a society that has consistently denied that identity. The ability to stand up to the truth or history is the power of the powerless. And it works because the powerful cannot erase the reality of human experience. I think this validity is what we see in so much of Zora Neale Hurston's work, in so many of her stories. Permit me to suggest that many critics miss the truth of human experience in her work, because their focus is not on the woman in the story, and because they are blinded by their opinions of protest literature. In *Jonah's Gourd Vine*, Lucy, the wife of John Pearson the preacher, is a perfect picture of a wife who does her best to stand by her man, or perhaps to stand behind her man. But as my sisters of Spelman remember my saying when I was there, and I continue to say at Bennett College for Women, the problem with a woman standing behind her man is she can't see where she is going.

And so Lucy is a perfect picture of a wife who chooses to stand behind her man in spite of his womanizing, but in the end on her deathbed she finds the strength to tell him off. The preacher, who has always been a weak man although he is the center of the story, is shown against the background of Lucy's long-suffering life. In the end she leaves him with massive guilt from which he never recovers. And so Sister Lucy has the last word after all. The power Lucy has is that of a woman who does not traditionally honor a male approach to struggle. And I put that as something that is not carried on the chromosome but something learned, and acknowledge that some men also do not honor a traditional male approach to struggle. Lucy's answer to oppression is in waiting patiently, the waiting of the righteous. And, like Delia in *Swept*, she strikes back, but only when the time is right.

As Zora collects the bones of women's experiences and sings over them, we are enlightened as to the lives of oppressed women about whom she writes, whose stories she tells, whose voices she becomes. She travelled the South and collected her work. Her research revealed to her how women were denied a voice in the church, or as we put it, the 'chuch'. How women were denied a voice in the community, and how woman were even denied a voice on the store's front porch where all the stories were told. Being denied a voice, they were denied the self-definition that stories can bring. Her characters spoke their own protests within her stories. For wolf woman, life can be a very solitary and lonely experience. It is a life that requires courage and determination.

And Zora's courage is impressive. Her own childhood could be understood to be a training ground for becoming tough and resilient as well as fearless. She was forced by circumstances and her mother's death as a teenager to adapt rapidly to a great many changes in her life. She says in *Dust Tracks on a Road* she was shifted from house to house of relatives and friends and found comfort nowhere. Her access to books was limited and that was misery, sheer misery, for Zora. By 14, she was working as a lady's maid and she learned early to move from here to there. At the age of 15, she was working for a theater troupe on her own. In her adult life, she often depended on the generosity of her friends for her survival. She did what she had to do, but was always true to her passion to write. Sometimes this meant poverty, sometimes it meant placating her painter, Godmother Mason. She lived her life piece by piece, but she got the writing done in spite of living from dime to dime.

Zora's writing was her life and she tried to speak for those who had no voice in the annals of history or 'herstory'. Her life's work has not been wasted. She has daughters everywhere. From Alice Walker to Ntozake Shange. From Toni Cade Bambara to

Toni Morrison, to the young women in our high schools and colleges, and those of you who write on, Zora's mark is there. For you write, too, I suspect, about women who, like Janie, find their voices through rebellion and pure nerve. If so, Zora is your foremother. The main conflict in her life was also the conflict of those she wrote about: the conflict between the freedom of the spirit and somebody's attempt to control your spirit. Folks who want to get your 'stuff'. Whether acted out in race, gender, or class issues, like our classic blues singers, Zora sang to express her own pain and to assert that, finally, the lives of the poor and the oppressed and, yes, of her sisters, do matter. Her life of running to be herself and to live her own life authentically earned her not only a place in literary history, but also a life of difficult and continuous struggle.

Had she chosen to marry the man she seemed to have loved above all others, Dr. Percy Parker, she could have lived in material comfort, but she feared that marriage to him would remove her from her life's work which, by its very nature, was not compatible with traditional marriage. And so the wild woman within her led her to Jamaica, to Haiti, and to the Deep South to experience firsthand, and to leave for us, the intricacies, the beauty, the pain, and the joy of black culture. Her greatest trial and the most severe test of her strength came to her without warning, when she was unjustly accused of child molestation in September 1948, Zora said, "That was the blow that knocked me loose from all that I have ever looked to and cherished." This blow was closely followed in January by another attempt to slander her when she refused to perjure herself for a white man in Los Angeles who knew one of Zora's friends. He had threatened her with a smear campaign if she would not lie for him. He accused her of owing him money. He accused her of indecent exposure. He accused her of smoking marijuana. And Zora Neale Hurston's treatment by the black press regarding these scandals was damaging and intensely cruel. It makes me remember a line (at least it is attributed to Zora Neale Hurston) she probably would have said of those members of the black press, a line we could well, my brothers and sisters, say today, "All my skinfolk ain't my kinfolk."

Arna Bontemps and Langston Hughes gossiped with each other about "One of our leading ladies of color getting in jail." Their reaction was less than sympathetic. One wonders how much the black press and those two poets enjoyed the disgrace of this black woman who was, yes, irreverent, outspoken, and not willing to fit anyone's definition of what a black woman should be. We must wonder whether a married woman would have been made so easy a target of such an attack. Suspicion has ever lain more heavily on single woman with no children and no man to belong to. Zora was exonerated after an excruciating year and when both slanderous campaigns were over, she moved to Miami and slowly pulled herself together after a very deep depression.

She kept writing articles in magazines almost until the end of her life, publishing over 21 articles from 1952 to the last one in 1959, the year before she died. Her last big project was the life of Herod the Great which did not see publication. Zora's strong independent spirit made her reluctant to go to a nursing home even after she suffered a stroke that disabled her. She had strong spiritual beliefs. Indeed, in those painful moments for my friends, my family, and myself, when death comes to fetch someone, I find myself writing for comfort words that Zora Neale Hurston wrote. She wrote that "Nothing is destructible. Things merely change forms. When the consciousness we know as life ceases, I know that I shall still be part and parcel of the world. I am one with the infinite and need no other assurance." Zora as wolf woman will be here, not only in Eatonville. Zora as wolf woman will be everywhere eternally. Her Daughters of the Dust carry on collecting and preserving the treasures she gave us, creating and recreating the stuff of her stories to which she so courageously dedicated her life. Who knows? Who knows but that one evening, the wild women who are her daughters will sing over her bones so beautifully that Zora will rise and vanish into the woods, laughing at life, and alive once more among us.

Thank you.

Sam Rivers and the Rivbea Orchestra.

Broadcast journalist Tracy Moore interviews N.Y. Nathiri.

Youth group at the Main stage.

Songwriter and musician Isaac Hayes

Education Day activities include gardening (foreground) and hands
on art (background).

Maurice J. O'Sullivan, professor of literature, Rollins College

A Basin in the Mind

Brian R. Owens

Artist Brian R. Owens creates oil paintings, drawings, and pastels, but is best known for his bronze sculptures. Owens won the "Best of Show" award in the juried art competition at the third annual Zora Neale Hurston Festival of the Arts and Humanities in 1992. Later that year, his work was exhibited at the Zora Neale Hurston National Museum of Fine Arts in Eatonville. Brian Owen's best known works include the bronze memorial sculpture honoring the civil rights activities of the St. Augustine Foot Soldiers, and the life-size bronze sculpture of educator Herald Parker for the Birmingham City Board of Education in Alabama.

Like most people, I am attracted to Zora Neale Hurston's image and apparent attitude: her knowing smile, her attention to style, her confidence. One doesn't have to read her novels to suspect, I think correctly, that she was ahead of her time. The iconic black-and-white photos of Zora are not unlike those that artists like myself take of themselves, carefully composed to show the most flattering angle. In her photos we see no evidence of struggle. That probably suits most of us just fine, accustomed as we are to the manner in which stories are delivered to us in movies and television. Our electronic hallucinations tend to follow predictable patterns. After suffering intensely, the heroine's victory is absolute, her enemies lay at her feet and the price she is made to pay is measured in stitches and fallen friends. But to study Zora's life is to study the truth of our world and to study the strategies and tactics that yielded a glorious life lived in constant struggle; a struggle within her mind and without. She was arguably victorious but hers was a bitter-sweet victory more like the tragedy of a Greek myth than a screenplay.

I'm not being negative. A realistic appraisal of my life and the forces at work around me is part of my system of survival. I look at Zora's life through the same lens. I don't need another object lesson in positive thinking. I just want to see things clearly. So why do I, an early 21st century working visual artist, care about Zora Neale Hurston? Because her life and work have helped sharpen the unknowable mental tools that I rely on to move my career forward. Because there are direct lessons useful to this visual artist to be drawn from her life story.

Usually, the writer and visual artist begin their professional lives with no money, no experience and no clout. Then they proceed to make something for which there is no immediate demand. To produce good literature and artwork is impressive in itself. To arrange one's life as she did, so what is done to pay the bills also produces source material for writing and sends one to the corners of the world that inform the writing, is brilliant. The culture instructs us that our human worth is connected to our material wealth. It smiles upon an adventurous life only if one observes its maxim to consume. But to negotiate one's own deals as she did, avoiding the traditional jobs that would deliver material wealth at the expense of the adventure in life is a sign of resourcefulness and flexibility of mind.

At the very beginning of my artistic adventure, I realized that I did not posses the tools necessary to live entirely from the sale of my art. For visual artists like myself, the odds against doing this are roughly ten thousand to one. This was the commonly accepted statistic back in the early 90s when times were good. Despite my education, skill, support and savings, I soon felt outmatched by the challenge. The aforementioned attributes would be necessary but insufficient ingredients to succeed. There are just too many critical forces at work beyond the control of the artist.

For the writer and visual artist the creative process is often uneven. Leonard Cohen acknowledged this reality when he said, "As a writer, you have to show up and go to work every day. But you do so knowing that today it may not come. That you are not in command of this enterprise." Creating a body of exemplary work is just the first step. At the beginning of my career, my working assumption was that there were enough opportunities within an eight-hour drive from my studio to support me. The challenge was to sharpen my vision and increase my connectivity with the world to help me identify these opportunities. In truth, I did not know exactly how to make this happen. But I knew it had something to do with changing the lens through which I saw the world and changing the way that I thought. I decided that filling in large missing gaps of knowledge that had nothing directly to do with sculpture and painting would make for a good start. Zora's work, along with other works of literature, helped me begin to fill in the gaps. In my imagination I saw this new knowledge swirling above an apparatus in my mind that I could not inspect but could still influence to my advantage. An apparatus where thoughts are tools.

In many ways Zora was my polar opposite. How strange it was, for me to identity with a woman whom Fannie Hurst (a friend of philanthropists in New York City) described as having "the gift of walking into hearts." And yet, we had some things in common: The "cosmic loneliness," as she put it, of being so different from her childhood friends; the decision against marriage; the disinterest in having children; the late start in the pursuit of vaulting dreams; the closeness she felt to her mother; the gulf between herself and her father.

During an interview, Christopher Hitchens quipped, "It is the death of the father that provides the son with an unobstructed view of his own grave and a little sign that says *you're next*." The death of my father left me with the constant awareness of the lightness and transience of all things and a willingness to take even greater personal risks on the theory that I'm not getting out of this thing alive anyway. If Zora were here, I might inquire about her unobstructed view. According to biographer Valerie Boyd, the death of Zora's father allowed her to close an excruciating chapter of life, leaving her freer and lighter at a point when her capabilities as a writer had reached a high level.

If Zora were here I would ask her if she played chess, given the apparent efficacy of her professional strategies and tactics. But in chess the strategy is to advance one's army and capture the opponent's King. Its underlying assumption is that one has power to begin with. Zora's maneuverings, however, may bear a closer resemblance to the ancient Chinese game of Go, in which the player starts with next to nothing and builds power over time; where there is no frontline and it is often difficult to evaluate the strength of one's position; where the object is to gradually hold more territory than one's opponent, territory that may not be completely controlled. The winner is determined when the players no longer wish to continue or when one player resigns for it is a game played with no set end.

The account of Zora's life triggers old memories and provokes interesting reflections. I remember what playwright David Mamet said about one of his characters whose theoretical knowledge was painfully tested in the foggy, unpredictable arena of real life: "Every lesson is driven home with such force ... inescapable force ... the real question is ... can you get something from it? Can you look at it?" I like to think that Zora's successes were a consequence, in part, of being able to look at a new lesson even as it sent her sailing through the ropes. This isn't about positive thinking or "following your bliss." It's about checking yourself. It's about seeing your situation clearly and understanding – to the degree possible - the motives of the often mysterious, mercurial human beings moving around on the same field as yourself, both friend and foe. This is easier to say than do and Zora had a talent for it that she parlayed into income and scholarly opportunities.

Her glorious creative and scientific capabilities matured just as the Great Depression pulled this nation into an abyss and ground the Harlem Renaissance and the dreams of many of her associates into bits. Her most painful experience with racism occurred in the heart of the metropolis in which she invested her greatest hope. She would die, never knowing that the world would claim her as its daughter. And yet, I've found no evidence of self-pity or anything bordering on it during her adulthood. Given the times she lived in, she appears to have been a strange sort of realist. Say what you will about hip hop musician/producer "50 cent." He touched on the subject of realism in a book he recently co-authored. If Zora were here, I wouldn't be surprised to see her nod her head in agreement with his maxim, "Your first task is to resist the temptation to wish you lived in a world that was fair."

If Zora were here, I would tell her about the times I spent in the city of her childhood; of the many books that keep company with hers on my shelf authored by the likes of Henry Miller, Octavia Butler and Fyodor Dostoyevsky. If she seemed receptive, I would tell her of my own vaulting ambitions. I'd tell her that of all my tools the most important one is the one forever hidden from view; the one that grew sharper and saw farther as I tried to perceive the world through the eyes of my fellow beings; the tool, refined by literature including her own, that preserved this working visual artist at the end of the American century and exists, as she put it: in "a basin in the mind where words float around on thoughts" and deeper still, where thoughts are "untouched by words."

Artist Brian Owens

Actor Charles S. Dutton (center)

Judges of the student competition at Universal Studios

White face dancers

Jose B. Fernandez, Dean of the UCF College of Arts and Humanities and Rosalyn Howard, UCF Associate Professor of Anthropology

Writer Valerie Boyd and actress Elizabeth Van Dyke

Actress Phylicia Raschad (center)

Arts and crafts at the Outdoor Festival

A scene from Zora Neale Hurston's *From Sun to Sun: A Day in the Life of a Railroad Camp.*

Panel discussion on Communities

Actor Ossie Davis

CONCLUSION

Reflections from ZORA! Celebrating 25 Years of the Zora Neale Hurston Festival of the Arts and Humanities

Benjamin D. Brotemarkle

Ben Brotemarkle is Executive Director of the Florida Historical Society. As a broadcast journalist, Dr. Brotemarkle has been covering the Zora Neale Hurston Festival of the Arts and Humanities since the first event in 1990. He has written about Eatonville, Zora Neale Hurston, and the festival in his books, including Beyond the Theme Parks: Exploring Central Florida, *and* Crossing Division Street: An Oral History of the African American Community in Orlando. *Under his direction, the Florida Historical Society has become very active in the ZORA! Festival, providing educational exhibits, author presentations, and the theatrical production* Female Florida: Historic Women in Their Own Words.

From its inception in 1990, the Zora Neale Hurston Festival of the Arts and Humanities has been a carefully conceived and well organized event that stimulates the senses and the intellect. The Association to Preserve the Eatonville Community, Inc. (P.E.C.), exposes festival attendees to academic giants, artistic geniuses, and other creative thinkers of African descent through lectures and panel discussions, visual and performing arts presentations, and a vibrant outdoor festival with diverse vendors. This internationally celebrated event promotes a sense of community for the residents of Eatonville, while inviting everyone to pull up a seat on Joe Clark's "lying porch" and make themselves at home.

Established in 1887, the historic town of Eatonville is the oldest incorporated African American municipality in the United States. This fact alone provides a firm foundation for excellent public history outreach opportunities. Writer, folklorist, and anthropologist Zora Neale Hurston was a celebrated figure of the Harlem Renaissance, and arguably the most significant cultural figure to come from Central Florida. The fact that Hurston called historic Eatonville "home" expands the opportunities for exceptional humanities-based programming even further. Through the Zora Neale Hurston Festival of the Arts and Humanities, P.E.C. is utilizing to the fullest extent the outstanding historic and cultural materials available to them.

Poet and performing artist Maya Angelou has written more than two dozen award winning books including *I Know Why the Caged Bird Sings*, *All God's Children Need Traveling Shoes*, and *Gather Together in My Name*. Maya Angelou praises the ZORA! Festival:

> This festival has a singular importance. It is not a festival in New York City or in Hollywood. It's not a festival in Chicago, or any of the big metropoli of the world. It's in Eatonville, Florida. And it is singular in that the festival—its existence itself—educates. Without a person even having to come here, he or she is forced to recognize this was the first incorporated all black town in the United States. That's fantastic to know. Many black people don't know that there were any. Not to mention whites, or Spanish-speaking or Native American. So it has a singular importance. Now then, of course, the larger importance or maybe the more glamorous and attractive importance—that it brings together these people who have achieved and we get a

chance to say to the young people "steady on, come on" you know, and "do it" and "we believe in you" and all the good things. It really is remarkable in and of itself. And so, the conveners have had great dreams. This is a very ambitious project.

Zora Neale Hurston is best remembered for her 1937 novel *Their Eyes Were Watching God*, the story of Janie Crawford and her attempts at self-realization. Hurston's other novels include *Jonah's Gourd Vine*, the story of an unfaithful man with an understanding wife; *Moses: Man of the Mountain*, a retelling of the biblical story of Moses; and *Seraph on the Suwanee*, Hurston's only book that features white people as main characters. As an anthropologist who studied under the renowned Franz Boas, Hurston published two collections of folklore, *Mules and Men* and *Tell My Horse*. Hurston also wrote dozens of short stories, essays, and dramatic works.

During the first quarter century of the Zora Neale Hurston Festival of the Arts and Humanities, a wide variety of academics, writers, visual artists, musicians, actors, dancers, and other creative thinkers have expressed how the work of Zora Neale Hurston has inspired them. Maya Angelou said that she first read Hurston's work in the 1940s and has continued to revisit it ever since:

> Miss Hurston's work encouraged me and informed me and did all the things that great literature must do for the species. I find it impossible to say where, you know, that her dialogue or her prose or her immediacy — because she uses a lot of language that is absolutely immediate — what those facets of her work has impressed or influenced me. I read everything. And I don't take a book and say "ahh — okay from this I'm going to get alliteration," you see, or "in this particular instance I'm going to look for imagery." I don't do that. I simply read. Just take it, put it in the brain. So I couldn't

say exactly how, but I know that she is a major influence in my life.

Actress Ruby Dee has appeared in numerous stage, film, and television productions, including the play *A Raisin in the Sun*, the film *Do the Right Thing*, and the screen adaptation of *Their Eyes Were Watching God*. As part of the first annual ZORA! Festival, Ruby Dee conducted an acting workshop at Rollins College. During a break in the workshop, she discussed what makes Hurston's writings noteworthy:

> The thing that really intrigues about Zora is that she recognized that our intellectuals, our giant imaginations, our brilliant people weren't necessarily the scholars and the middle class. She knew that found in the back woods are extraordinary people, who never heard of Ibsen, who are capable of putting the universe in perspective— genius storytellers who could put the elements of life into imaginative contexts, who might not be able to spell or read and write.

Actor, singer, and songwriter Oscar Brown, Jr. appeared in the American Playhouse Theater production of *Zora is My Name: The Zora Neale Hurston Story*, the television series *Brewster Place*, and many stage productions. He has directed, produced, and composed musicals including the Broadway production of *Big Time Buck White*, *Joy 66*, *Summer in the City of Chicago*, and *Slave Song*. Brown has written hundreds of songs, collaborating with jazz legend Miles Davis and Brazilian songwriter Luis Enrique. Oscar Brown, Jr. says that Zora Neale Hurston and her work has had a profound impact on him:

> I consider myself in Zora Neale Hurston's spirit. I was long before I even heard of her. I've been trying to do some of the same kinds of things that she did—to reflect, as accurately as I could through my writing,

what I heard, what I saw around me. I felt that was every bit as exotic and interesting and beautiful as any other culture. That was particularly true at the point when I started writing seriously back in the late '50s and '60s, when there was a folk song craze. People were singing stuff from all kinds of cultures. I said, "Why not the ally back there in Chicago?" My act, so to speak, is based on that sort of thing and bits of folklore which I gathered, to which I have to talk my hat off to Zora Neale Hurston, because I never heard of these characters until I read about them in her writings.

Elizabeth Van Dyke toured the country in the one-woman show *Zora Neale Hurston* by Lawrence Holder, and has helped to stage several theatrical productions over the years at the ZORA! Festival. In 1933, Zora Neale Hurston staged her play *From Sun to Sun: A Day in the Life of a Railroad Camp* at Rollins College, near Eatonville. At the ZORA! Festivals in 1993 and 1994, Elizabeth Van Dyke directed a reconstructed version of *From Sun to Sun* on the same college campus, but in a different venue:

> In 1933, the Annie Russell Theater did not allow blacks in the theater, so she could not do *From Sun to Sun* there. She had to do it at the Recreation Hall, where no blacks were allowed to attend. In 1993, here we are, full force, in the Annie Russell Theater. It is a great honor and a great responsibility. It is very fitting because Zora was about claiming your history, claiming your legacy. Here we are in 1993, reliving this, and hopefully passing it on to a new generation.

Deloris Purdie was a featured performer in both the 1993 and 1994 productions of *From Sun to Sun: A Day in the Life of a Railroad Camp*. At the ZORA! Festival in 2011, Deloris Purdie played the role of Zora Neale Hurston in the Florida Historical Society (FHS) theatrical production *Female Florida: Historic Women in Their Own*

Words. Purdie also portrayed Hurston in the FHS documentary *The Lost Years of Zora Neale Hurston,* broadcast across the country on public television stations. Deloris Purdie's portrayal of Zora Neale Hurston in *Female Florida* is based on the 1928 essay *How it Feels to be Colored Me.* Hurston describes her childhood in Eatonville, and how it helped to form her progressive views on race. Although Hurston's Harlem Renaissance contemporaries wanted her to be angrier about the plight of African Americans, Purdie points out that Hurston refused:

> There was no need for her to be angry, because she knew who she was, and she knew where she had come from, and how her mother had raised her with all the confidence and hope. And it's "Get up and do something," and if you do that, then the world is your oyster. She knew that, so nobody could touch her, in her mind, and that's all that matters.

Glenda Dickerson heads the Drama Department at Spelman College, and has participated in academic panel discussions at the Zora Neale Hurston Festival of the Arts and Humanities. Dickerson has also adapted Hurston's work for the stage. She remembers her first encounter with Zora Neale Hurston's work:

> In 1972, I was living in Washington, D.C., and I went into the People's Drug Store on Fourteenth Street, and I saw a novel that had a black woman on the cover. It cost ninety-five cents, and it was called *Their Eyes Were Watching God.* So I bought it, not thinking anything about it. I read it, and my life was transformed. At the time I had been asked to direct a show at Theater Lobby in Washington, and I asked if instead of doing the show they wanted, if I could do an adaptation of this novel. That's how my production of *Jump at the Sun* came to the stage. Both Alice Walker and Angela Davis, who were in the house when we opened it in San Francisco, said to me that they thought that it was the definitive production of *Their Eyes Were Watching God.* So it transformed my life, the lives of the cast, and the lives of the people who saw it.

Playwright George C. Wolfe has adapted three of Hurston's short stories into the show *Spunk*. Wolfe directed the very successful Broadway shows *Angels in America, Jelly's Last Jam*, and *Bring in 'da Noise, Bring in 'da Funk*, and he has produced the New York Shakespeare Festival. After speaking at the ZORA! Festival in 1994, Wolfe said about Zora Neale Hurston:

> She's a great American artist, and we in this country have an incredibly sloppy tradition of honoring artists. I think when you are a black artist in this country, there's an added element of race, but by and large in this entire country there's a fundamental disregard for the quality of what artists bring to and put into their work. In Japan, they think of artists as living treasures. We don't have that phenomenon, but we're trying to cultivate that. Zora Neale Hurston is a great American author, the way Hawthorne, Hemingway, and Fitzgerald are great American authors. She needs to be deified because she contributed to and transformed the landscape of American literature. Her work has transformed the world. It's a phenomenon of racism in this country that you denigrate something and at the same time export it around the world. That duality needs to end. The more that African American people can claim with arrogance their culture, the less that phenomenon is going to happen.

The work of Zora Neale Hurston is gaining recognition around the world, and the Zora Neale Hurston Festival of the Arts and Humanities attracts an international audience far beyond her hometown of Eatonville. Irina Morozova is Professor of Literature at Russian State University in Moscow, and participated with two of her students in the 2013 ZORA! Festival. Morozova first encountered Hurston's work as a Fulbright Scholar at the University of Central Florida. Before her studies at UCF, Morozova had never heard of Hurston, but was very impressed with *Their Eyes Were Watching God* and other work. Morozova dedicated herself to exposing her students, and the general public in Russia, to the writings of Zora Neale Hurston through special courses and a web site:

> I was raised in Soviet school and Soviet University and at that time our favorite African American writers were like Richard Wright, James Baldwin, you know, all these writers with social revolt, protest, and so on and so forth, and I thought that all African American literature is like that. So Zora Hurston, that was my new discovery of America, you know, really, and that was so, so different. So, that's why I decided I needed to do something with that.

Preserving African American history and culture is at the heart of the ZORA! Festival. In 1992, Dorothy Porter Wesley participated in a panel discussion called "Protectors of the Heritage." In 1930, Dorothy Porter Wesley was asked to assemble a collection of resource materials by and about people of African descent for Howard University. Because of the lack of existing printed materials focusing on African Americans, Wesley explored the attics and basements of people's homes, collecting newspaper clippings, letters, tax reports, and other materials to make historical information available to scholars. While working on her extensive research project, Wesley met Zora Neale Hurston at a dinner party:

> She came to Howard in 1924 and '25, and I didn't come until 1928, so I missed her. When she was visiting Washington one day, we were both invited to dinner by a book collector named Henry Slaughter. Something happened in the kitchen, and dinner wasn't ready until eleven. I had all evening to listen to Zora Neale Hurston's tales. She had so many of them I just couldn't believe it, They were so unique and unusual. I thought she was a very interesting character.

Since 1990, the Zora Neale Hurston Festival of the Arts and Humanities has offered academic discussions and scholarly presentations, concerts, visual art exhibitions, theatrical performances, and a three-day "outdoor festival" featuring African American crafts, music, books, storytelling, memorabilia, and food during the last week of January. Festival participant Maya Angelou praises ZORA! Festival's mission of historic preservation in Eatonville:

> All people need to know their heritage. A person who doesn't know where he's been has very little chance of charting where he or she is going. You must know. And I do believe that people live in direct relation to the heroes and sheroes they have, always and in all ways. And all those people who went before, and paid for you, Mr. Brotemarkle, and for me, need to be cherished. Just the grace of saying "thank you" increases and enriches our present lives and prepares us to enrich the lives of those who are yet to come. It is very clear.

To present a consistently excellent annual event such as the Zora Neale Hurston Festival of the Arts and Humanities over a quarter century requires the hard work and dedication of many individuals. The board of directors, staff, and volunteers of the Association to Preserve the Eatonville Community, Inc. (P.E.C.) should be commended on this remarkable accomplishment, along with the festival's National Planning Committee. A wide variety of other organizations including Rollins College, the University of Central Florida, the Maitland Art Center, the Orlando Museum of Art, the Florida Historical Society, and many others have served as valuable partners for this event. Every ship needs a captain, though, and from the beginning, the leader of the ZORA! Festival has been Mrs. N.Y. Nathiri. Just a few weeks before the Twenty-Fifth Annual Zora Neale Hurston Festival of the Arts and

Humanities was to take place, N.Y. Nathiri was already looking ten years into the future of the event:

> We have some very important milestones coming at us. For example, 2016 will be the 125th birthday of Zora Neale Hurston, and we're looking already to have a year-long commemoration, yes, in Eatonville, in Washington, D.C. at Howard University, in New York City because of the Harlem experience. We are looking in 2019 to work with scholars in Japan to do a festival program there. Now, of course, 2015 will be significant to us because it begins that next cycle of five years. What festival has done increasingly over the years is to set a kind of course for what we will be doing organizationally. For us at this festival, the ZORA STEM Initiative—science, technology, engineering, and math—the initiative that the organization Preserve Eatonville Community is launching with this festival will be a ten year initiative, research based, with scholars at the University of Central Florida, under the lead of Dr. Pamela McCauley-Bush and the College of Engineering. We are looking to really solidify our contribution to the revitalization of the historic Eatonville community and that is about preparing students in Eatonville and elsewhere to be able to assume the well-paying jobs of the 21st century.

The remarkable history of Eatonville and its most famous resident, Zora Neale Hurston, will continue to serve as a catalyst for historic preservation, cultural celebration, and community revitalization well into the future through the Zora Neale Hurston Festival of the Arts and Humanities.

Ben Brotemarkle collecting interviews in the early 1990s.

Actor, singer, songwriter Oscar Brown, Jr.

The Florida Historical Society outdoor festival tent.

A Florida Historical Society educational exhibit.

Deloris Purdie as Zora Neale Hurston in the Florida Historical
Society theatrical production *Female Florida: Historic Women in Their
Own Words*. (Alan Chapman Photography)

N.Y. Nathiri, Ruby Dee, Elizabeth Van Dyke

FHS Vice President Tracy Moore and community organizer Henry Moore at the Festival banquet.

The ZORA! Festival as seen from above.